BIGSHOTS, PIPSQUEAKS
& WINDBAGS

Also by Gene Perret

———————————————■———————————————

Gene Perret's Funny Business
(Written with Linda Perret)

■

Great One-Liners
(Written with Terry Perret)

BIGSHOTS, PIPSQUEAKS & WINDBAGS

JOKES, STORIES, & ONE-LINERS
ABOUT PEOPLE, POWER
& POLITICS

Gene Perret • Linda Perret

PRENTICE HALL
Englewood Cliffs, New Jersey 07632

Prentice-Hall International (UK) Limited, *London*
Prentice-Hall of Australia Pty. Limited, *Sydney*
Prentice-Hall Canada, Inc., *Toronto*
Prentice-Hall Hispanoamericana, S.A., *Mexico*
Prentice-Hall of India Private Limited, *New Delhi*
Prentice-Hall of Japan, Inc., *Tokyo*
Simon & Schuster Asia Pte. Ltd., *Singapore*
Editora Prentice-Hall do Brasil, Ltda., *Rio de Janeiro*

©1993 *by*
Gene Perret and Linda Perret

10 9 8 7 6 5 4 3 2 1

Library of Congress Cataloging-in-Publication Data

Perret, Gene.
  Bigshots, pipsqueaks & windbags : jokes, stories & one
liners about people, power & politics / Gene Perret and
Linda Perret.
    p. cm.
  Includes index.
  ISBN 0-13-350331-3
  1. American wit and humor. 2. Politics—Humor.
  3. Power—Humor.
  I. Perret, Linda. II. Title. III. Title: Bigshots, pipsqueaks,
and windbags.
PN6162.P39   92-34383
818′.5402—dc20   CIP

ISBN   0-13-350331-3

PRENTICE HALL
Professional Publishing
Englewood Cliffs, NJ 07632
Simon & Schuster, A Paramount Communications Company

Printed in the United States of America

to
Wendy and Heidi

———————■———————

to
Adam Lux,
who I know is in
a place filled with laughter

CONTENTS

Part one

PEOPLE

"People have one thing in common:
they are all so different."
—Robert Zend

1   AT WORK

2   AT LARGE

Part two

POWER

"A friend in power is
a friend lost."

— Henry Adams

3 AT WORK

4 AWAY FROM WORK

Part three

POLITICS

> "Being in politics is like being
> a football coach. You have to
> be smart enough to understand
> the game and stupid enough to
> think it's important."
>
> —Eugene McCarthy

5 THE OVERALL PICTURE

6 THE PEOPLE OF GOVERNMENT

7 GETTING ELECTED TO GOVERNMENT

8 THE PERKS OF POLITICS

9 THE COST OF GOVERNMENT

10 THE PROBLEMS OF GOVERNMENT

11 GOVERNMENT AGENCIES

12 GOVERNMENT GONE AWRY

FROM THE AUTHORS

There's a cadence to comedy just as there is a rhythm to music. The beat is as much a part of a song as the melody and the lyrics. So, too, the tempo of a one-liner is essential to the humor. Tampering with that meter can destroy the overall effect.

That's why we've avoided some of today's devices for genderless writing. Using *his or her* or *a person* to replace a pronoun throws off the meter of the line, often ruining the comedy impact in the process.

Where there was a choice, we decided to go with the masculine pronoun rather than alternate. This was for consistency and not to make any sexist statement.

Good humor is universal and we intended that the fun in these pages apply equally to men and women. Readers can easily substitute the appropriate gender and still retain the comedy and the entertainment of this book.

AUTHORS' INTRODUCTION

Monday mornings are traumatic. You have to get up and go to you-know-where (your office) to do you-know-what (work). Terrible!

But wait a minute. Your workplace isn't that bad. It's probably in a higher-priced neighborhood than your house. The lighting is better, and for the most part, the chairs are more comfortable. Well, the chairs are more comfortable if you're high enough up the executive ladder. In general, though, you'd have to admit that the workplace isn't more of a hardship than being home—except you do have to work there.

But wait another minute. Work isn't that insufferable, either. It's not backbreaking work; it's not slave labor. In fact, if it's not downright fun, at least it's something to do. When you do it well, you feel a sense of accomplishment. Don't forget, too, that you get paid for it. That's more than you can say about mowing the lawn, changing the light bulbs, cleaning out the garage, or chastising the children—all the fun things you enjoyed during the weekend.

Then why is going to work so universally dreaded? Because the workplace is populated with people. Aha! There's the number-one problem—people.

The first harrowing trauma that you and I face going back to work on Monday is the drive there. Why? Because there are other cars on the road, and each one of those irritating automobiles has at least one person in it. Idiots change lanes in front of us; imbeciles tailgate behind us; morons go slow when we want to go fast; and lamebrains go too fast when we're driving at a safe rate of speed.

Think what an enjoyable ride to work this would be if there were no other people. You'd see and enjoy more scenery. You could change lanes whenever you wanted, without even checking the rearview mirror. You could talk on your car phone without having to worry about rear ending some nitwit who stops suddenly, although I'm not quite sure whom you would talk to. It would be a pleasant jaunt.

When you get to your office, you could park anywhere you wanted. Suppose you came up to a parking place that was marked "Reserved for Mr. Cudahy"; park there. There is no Mr. Cudahy.

And if you're Mr. Cudahy, that's even better. You don't have to fret that some inconsiderate buffoon is going to be parked in your parking space.

Nice, isn't it?

The next trauma is when you get to the office and you pick up all those pink slips, your phone messages, with some trepidation. Any one of those could announce that the big deal you were basing your future on has fallen through. Any one of them could tell you that your insurance rates are going up, your taxes are being audited, the principal wants you to come to the office to discuss a problem with little Johnny. They've arranged for a police car to pick you up and drive you to the school at 1:30 this afternoon. You don't have to worry about those now because there are no messages. There are no people. Who could call?

There will be no angry messages on your answering machine from the boss. There is no boss. There are no fellow workers with annoying habits because there are no fellow workers.

Isn't work without people pleasant? Of course, one drawback is that you'll have to make your own coffee, but that's a small price to pay for the luxury of being alone in the workplace.

People can be a nuisance even away from the office. When you try to relax and enjoy yourself, it's people who talk all through the movie you're trying to enjoy. At a party, there's always some loudmouth making a fool of himself. It's a person. People are the primary peeve of the business world.

Who can be even more grating than people? People with power. Your normal, everyday, commonplace, off-the-rack people are bothersome enough, but people who have the authority to tell you what to do, when to do it, whom to do it with—those are the ones who really can make your skin crawl.

And you meet plenty of those during your workday, too. How about the police officer who pulls you over just for going too fast, for exceeding the posted limit. Sure you were going fast, but you have an important job and it's imperative that you get to the office fast. Why doesn't this public servant leave you alone and chase the real criminals—the people with not-so-important jobs who insist on cutting in front of you on the freeways? They're the ones who should be cited and put behind bars.

How about the cop at the intersection that is under repair? He stops you—you, of all people—and lets insignificant, lower- class people drive by.

You're constantly confronting people with a little authority who don't understand what an important cog you are in the corporate world. There's the receptionist who holds the keys to the inner sanctum—the office of the client you're calling on. She could say, "Go right in, Ms. Big Shot is waiting for you," but no, she says, "Have a seat, please."

There's the maitre d' at the important restaurant who refuses to give you the important table, the flight attendant who tells you, "Sit down and put your seat belt on and don't stand up again until the captain announces that the aircraft is safely parked at the gate." Hasn't anyone told her that those signs are for the other people, for hoi polloi? You, because of your lofty position within Corporate America, have been given a dispensation from obeying safety regulations.

You're constantly harassed by little people with a little authority. Power is the second great peeve of the business world.

Then there's the ultimate power, the power that we freely give to people under the guise of democracy. That power is political power. It is the most frustrating of all because it cloaks itself in the guise of service. Those who have it wield it for our own good. At least, that's their story.

Their sworn duty, they say, is to rob from the rich and give to the poor. They also take a cut of the action.

No matter what work you do, you're forced to consider government regulations, and they're always troublesome. If they weren't, they wouldn't need a statute to enforce them.

You have to pay taxes, do things you don't want to do, do things that it makes no sense to do, because some government bureaucrat or some law, ordinance, regulation, prescript, rule, decree, act, edict, legislation, or bylaw says that you must.

To paraphrase some wise man's saying: "Power is a pain. Absolute power is an absolute pain in the tail."

Politics is the third peeve of the businessperson.

Everyone who works for a living has to deal with people, contend with power, and endure the fruits of politics. Some say you can't fight City Hall, and they may be right. This book, though, offers one way of either fighting back or getting even. It offers some quips, one-liners, and anecdotes that may help soothe the beleaguered soul. If you can't cope with the three peeves of the business world—people, power, and politics—you can at least laugh at them.

Enjoy.

Part One

PEOPLE

"People have one thing in common:
they are all so different."

Robert Zend

Chapter 1

AT WORK

THE COMPANY MAN

There's one guy in our office who believes the company can do no wrong. How can he believe that? They hired him, didn't they?

■

Some workers believe their company can do no wrong. If they had their way, they'd keep a vigil light burning in front of the Quality Control Department.

■

One guy in our office insists "I work for the best company in the entire world." I said, "No company that you work for could ever finish higher than second place."

Some people automatically believe not only the company line, but also the hook and the sinker, too.

■

Some workers just automatically kiss the CEO's ring. Even if he keeps it in his back pocket.

■

One co-worker of mine says, "Whenever you speak of me, be sure to mention that I'm behind the company 100 percent." I say, "Whenever I speak of you, the word "behind" is generally in the same sentence."

■

One co-worker said, "What's good for the company is good for me." Then how come the company made $426 million last year and he has trouble making his car payments?

■

One guy used to treat the company as his "loving mother." When he got laid off, he tried to file for child abuse.

He went directly from working for his "loving mother" to collecting unemployment insurance at the "orphanage."

■

Many workers are married to the company ... and it's fooling around behind their back.

■

He's been with the company so long. When he started the Dead Sea was only sick.

THE COMPANY CRITIC

Every office has a loud-mouthed critic. You know, a guy who puts his foot in his mouth, but never far enough to keep it quiet.

■

One co-worker criticizes everything the company does. I said, "Why would you work for the worst company in the world?" He said, "They're the only ones who will have me."

This guy thinks our company is the worst company in the world. I said, "Anyone who thinks that is the worst employee in the world." He said, "Small world, isn't it?"

■

If the company says "black," he says "white." If the company says "up," he says "down." If the company says "raise," he says, "Thank you."
... he's a cynic; not an imbecile.

■

He believes the exact opposite of whatever the company decides. He thinks we should work Christmas Day and have the rest of the year off.

■

He thinks everyone above him in the company is an absolute jackass. I said, "If you honestly believe that, how can you go in and ask people like that for a raise?" He said, "They're just stupid enough to give it to me."

■

I said, "If you hate this company so much, how can you work here?" He said, "Oh, I don't work here. I'm just employed here."

■

This one guy criticizes everything the company does. He's like Siskel working for Ebert.

■

This guy criticizes everything the company does. If he were one of Santa's elves, he'd tell Santa to lose weight and shave.

■

The company critic should keep in mind Franklin P. Jones's words, "Honest criticism is hard to take, particularly from a relative, a friend, an acquaintance, or a stranger."

ALWAYS LATE

We have one guy who works in our office. The only time he's not late for work is when he's absent.

He's been late for work every day of his life, but he makes up for it by leaving early.

■

It's not his fault. He just moves slowly. In fact, he even stands still slowly.

■

This guy is late for everything. He didn't show up for his own wedding until two days into the honeymoon.

■

This guy would be late for his own funeral if it weren't for those six guys carrying him.

■

Normally when a person comes into the office everyone says, "Good morning." When this guy comes in everyone says, "Where do you want to go for lunch?"

■

The boss chastised him once. The boss said, "I get up at 5 o'clock sharp every morning because I learned as a young man that the early bird catches the worm. Now what does that teach you?" The guy said, "Not to come to your house for breakfast."

■

The boss warned him: "I want to see you at your desk, ready to go, pencil in hand at 8 o'clock tomorrow." Next day he was 20 minutes late. He said he had to stop on his way to work to buy a pencil.

■

This guy is just late for everything. The boss called him into his office to fire him. By the time he got there, the boss had been fired.

■

Another guy was late for everything but lunch and dinner meetings. He was on time only for things that had two cocktails in front of them.

■

There's one girl at the office who was always late because she couldn't find a parking space. By the time the boss figured out she didn't own a car, she could afford one.

There's a trick to not being late. Just set your clock 15 minutes ahead, and you'll never be late. Of course, you may get fired for leaving early.

■

If you are going to be late, be sure to have a good excuse ... unlike Ernie, who strolled into the office an hour late for the third time in a week. He found the boss awaiting him, "What's the story this time?" the boss asked sarcastically. "Let's hear a good excuse for a change."

Ernie explained, "Everything went wrong this morning, boss. My wife decided to drive me to the station. She got ready in ten minutes, but then the drawbridge got stuck. Rather than let you down, I swam across the river, ran out to the airport, got a hitch on a helicopter, landed on top of Radio City Music Hall, and was carried here piggy-back by one of the Rockettes."

"You'll have to do better than that, Ernie," said the boss, "No woman can get ready in ten minutes."

■

When Ms. Jones was asked if she had a good reason for always being late, she replied: "Yes, it makes the day seem shorter."

■

Punctuality is the ability to guess how late the boss is going to be.

FREQUENTLY ABSENT

Absenteeism is the worker's way of saying: "I don't know what you'd ever do without me, but today you're going to find out."

■

Absenteeism is getting paid for doing nothing. Of course, for some workers, that's also a day at the office.

■

One co-worker always takes the exact number of yearly sick days that the company allows. Apparently he keeps getting attacked by bugs who have read the contract.

One guy had the 48-hour flu and it lasted 51 hours. He not only took time off, but he tried to collect overtime for the three extra hours.

■

Another guy had the 24-hour virus, so he took three days off from work. He said he had it only during working hours.

■

One co-worker keeps calling in sick, but nobody really believes him. Instead of a get well card, we send him a "get real" card.

■

I feel sorry for one co-worker's grandmother. She has died on the first game of every World Series for the past 13 years.

■

One co-worker is absent so much that when he shows up at work everybody thinks something is wrong with him.

■

One guy in our office wants to be an undercover agent. That way when he's absent, who'll know?

■

One co-worker was absent so much that the first time he put in a complete week's work, we fired him. It was the only time we could really find out what he did.

■

We had a guy who was absent so much he celebrated his 25th anniversary with the company after 35 years.

■

Absence makes the heart grow fonder . . . except in business. In that case, absence makes one look yonder.

■

She's hardly at work. She comes in on Tuesday just to wish everybody a nice weekend.

THE CLOCK WATCHER

I had one co-worker who retired. As a going away gift the company gave him something he's had his eye on for a long time–the office clock.

■

One guy who worked in our office was an incurable clock watcher. If he had worked in Roman times, he would have been a sundial watcher.

■

The boss told us one day that we'd all have to keep our nose to the grindstone and our shoulders to the wheel. This guy refused to do it. He said he couldn't watch the clock from that position.

■

Some clock watchers have a lot of nerve. There was one whose boss was patiently explaining mistakes the employee had made during the day. Suddenly the employee interrupted her boss and said, "Ms. Johns, it's two minutes past five and you're annoying me on my own time."

■

This one guy had his eye on the clock so much that his face broke out in numbers.

■

We had this one guy in our office who did nothing but watch the clock. He retired, and two months later the clock died of loneliness.

■

I won't say this guy watches the clock a lot, but he went to the optometrist last week and found out his right eye now has a second hand.

■

One guy in our office actually cheers for quitting time. From 2 o'clock on he just sits there and says, "Go, clock, go."

One guy in our office says he just lives for quitting time. Although to look at him during working hours, you couldn't be at all sure that he was living.

■

That was his biggest disappointment during his entire working career—that he was limited to only one quitting time per day.

■

One guy in our office hates Friday afternoons because he knows it's almost three full days until the next quitting time.

■

She is a steady worker . . . hasn't missed a coffee break in ten years.

THE GOLDBRICKER

The true office goldbrick has a unique workplace. Instead of an "in" and "out" basket on his desk, he has an "in" and "stay in."

■

The office goldbrick also has an excellent safety record. It's hard to hurt yourself if you never move.

■

We have a goldbrick in our office who does absolutely nothing, but he does it fast.

■

The boss yells at him about once a month, but all that does is blow the cobwebs off his desk.

■

The boss got so angry at one office goldbrick he tried to fire him. But he couldn't relieve him of his duties because no one knew what they were.

■

The nice thing about being a goldbrick is that when you take a day off work, you don't fall behind.

The office goldbrick's motto is: "Ask not what you can do for your company. In fact, ask not anything."

■

I once worked with an office goldbrick who was actually stressed out. He said he had so much not to do he couldn't handle it.

■

We had one office goldbrick who was an absolute virtuoso. He retired from the company after 27 years with the same number of paper clips he started with.

■

Normally, at retirement parties the manager will read off a list of the retiree's accomplishments. At this guy's party we hired a pantomimist.

■

Looking for volunteers, the boss said, "I have an easy job for the laziest man on my staff. Will the laziest man please raise his hand?"
Instantly, all the employees raised their hands. All but one.
The boss walked over to his desk and asked, "Why didn't you raise your hand like everybody else?"
"Too much trouble." replied the man.

■

Bob Orben had a great line about a goldbricker. He said one worker was so lazy he was like a blister—didn't show up until all the work was done.

■

The goldbricker is a lot like the football player whose coach was putting the team through a tough workout. He had them doing sit-ups, push-ups, and finally the bicycle. This is an exercise that requires a player to lie on his back, legs up in the air, and move them as if he were riding a bike. "Is there a problem?" the coach asked one motionless player. "No problem," the player replied. "I'm coasting."

■

A woman went to the doctor complaining about not being able to perform as well at work. After a full examination and series of tests, the doctor came back with a diagnosis.

"The problem is you're just plain lazy," said the doctor.

"Okay," said the woman, "Just write down the medical term so I can give it to my supervisor."

THE SUNSHINE SPREADER

Every office has a "Sunshine Spreader." The first to take up a collection to buy a gift for any occasion. They're usually easy to spot—one of their hands is shaped like a cigar box.

■

As soon as anyone is sick, these people begin extracting money for a Get Well card and a gift. They're so aggressive that the lucky one is the person who's out sick.

■

Some office collectors are very persistent. If you don't have any change at the moment, they send you dunning notices.

■

We have one guy in our office who enjoys collecting so much we think he's a fallen-away toll-booth operator.

■

One guy in our office takes up so many collections his palms are sunburned.

■

This co-worker in our office loves to take up collections. I've worked with him 17 years and have never once seen him with his hands in his own pocket.

■

One lady in our office extracts so much money from us, she considers the Red Cross Bloodmobile a competitor.

■

They take up so many collections in my office that for the first three months I worked there I genuflected.

One guy in our office fainted and the office "Sunshine Spreader" had a bouquet of flowers on his desk before he hit the ground.

Of course, she did have some extra time in this case. He happened to fall out an open window.

■

W. C. Fields had a simple message for "Sunshine Spreaders": "Start every day off with a smile and get it over with."

■

The sunshine spreader always manages to see the bright side of your problem.

RABBLE ROUSERS

Every office has a troublemaker. He's easy to spot. He wears a shirt, a tie, and two little horns growing out of his head.

■

Troublemaking is in some people's blood. They're the kind of folks who would vote a town dry and then move.

■

Rabble rousers are the kind who will cause dissension in the office and then complain to the boss about unpleasant working conditions.

■

Rabble rousers like trouble. They consider office harmony a personal affront.

■

Rabble rousers like to spread disharmony in the office. They consider gnashing of teeth a sweeter sound than Muzak.

■

Rabble rousers like to see everyone in the office get along like brothers—Cain and Abel.

Rabble rousers like to start office feuds. They'd be perfectly happy if half the workers showed up wearing blue and the other half wearing gray.

■

One rabble rouser I knew was so good at turning employee against employee that if it hadn't been for the office nonsmoking rule, we would have burned each other in effigy.

■

Office rabble rousers should be nipped in the bud—or some other suitably vulnerable part of the body.

■

There are only two things I can't stand in the workplace— troublemakers and people who disagree with me.

■

The rabble rouser tends to be like the church lady who was accidentally overlooked when it came to be invited to the minister's garden party. The minister called at the last minute to apologize for his oversight and ask her to please attend.

"It's no use," the church lady said, "I've already prayed for rain."

RUMOR MONGER

You show me an office that doesn't have rumors floating through it, and I'll show you an office that's had its windows boarded up for three years.

■

An office rumor is fiction that hopes someday to grow up to be fact.

■

An office rumor is like a bridal shower. It's a big to-do over something that hasn't happened yet.

A rumor is like a head cold. As soon as some people get one, they can't wait to get rid of it.

■

Many office workers love a good rumor. It's something for them to believe in while they're waiting for it to happen.

■

One co-worker told me he knew this particular rumor was true; he started it.

■

One guy in our office hates rumors. So as soon as he hears one, he passes it to somebody else.

■

We have the world's greatest rumor monger in our office. The only time his tongue was ever still was when he got it caught in the top drawer of a filing cabinet.

■

This guy's tongue wags so much that if it were on the hind end of a cocker spaniel, it would win the "Miss Congeniality" title every year at the dog show.

■

This guy can't spread rumors fast enough. So he had his tongue Xeroxed.

■

There are some in the office who have the belief, "You can't believe everything you hear, but you can repeat it."

■

The rumor mongers are the ones who have surgery every couple of months . . . to remove a water cooler from their sides.

■

There are two reasons why some people don't mind their own business. One is that they haven't any mind, the other is that they haven't any business.

MEETING PERCUSSIONIST

Many executives get nervous and drum their fingers at meetings. Of course, we should be glad they didn't adopt athletes' nervous mannerisms—scratching their crotch and spitting.

■

One co-worker constantly taps his fingers. From the wrist down he thinks he's Fred Astaire.

■

One executive worked up such a sweat tapping away with his fingers, he finally developed athlete's fingernail.

■

There's only one thing more annoying than a person drumming while you're trying to think—and that's everyone else thinking while you're trying to drum.

■

A manager who called one meeting to order summed it up pretty well. She said, "At this meeting we'll have eight committee reports and one drum solo."

■

If executives have to have nervous habits at meetings, why couldn't they pick a quieter one—like thumb sucking?

■

Of course, some people you like to see tapping their fingers on the tabletop. It keeps their hands up where you can see them.

■

One co-worker vibrates his leg during the entire meeting. I don't know whether he's nervous or he's daydreaming that he's a dog and someone is scratching his belly.

■

One executive used to get so nervous at meetings he became a nail biter. Not just his own—anybody's.

Come to think of it, most meetings would be more endurable if the attendees had to check all movable body parts at the door.

■

The meeting percussionist is the one who can turn an hour meeting into eternity.

THE PERPETUAL SCREW-UP

We have a guy in our office who can do nothing right. He can't flush a toilet without an instruction manual.

■

They say there's a right way to do something and a wrong way. After this guy does it, there are two wrong ways.

■

This guy never makes the same mistake twice. The second time he does something, he always discovers a new mistake.

■

This guy had to give up sky diving because he could never remember which direction to go after he left the plane.

■

If you asked this guy for change of a nickel, he'd ask you how you wanted it.

■

There's a guy in our office who can't do anything right. He once got a paper cut unwrapping a Band-Aid.

■

This guy fouls up everything he touches. If he worked on the Dead Sea Scrolls, they'd come back to life again.

■

This guy doesn't know how to do anything. Once he wasted an entire hour trying to get a drink at the water cooler. He was looking for the coin slot.

This man destroys every project the boss gives to him. He's more effective than the office paper shredder.

■

We call this guy the office magician. With one phone call he can make customers disappear.

■

Mae West would have described the office screw-up as the kind of girl "who climbs the ladder of success wrong by wrong."

■

He makes so many mistakes, instead of an In & Out basket, he just has one that says "Oops."

■

The office screw-up is a little different from a computer. When a computer makes a mistake, it doesn't blame it on a co-worker.

■

The office screw-up is like a tea bag . . . he doesn't know his own strength until he's in hot water.

COFFEE DRINKER

We have a guy in our office who is a real coffee freak. I won't say this guy drinks too much coffee, but the last time he blinked was twelve years ago.

■

This guy drinks so much coffee his blood type is A-Columbian.

■

He has so much coffee in him, he doesn't burp; he percolates.

■

With the amount of coffee this guy drinks, you'd think by this time Juan Valdez could have gotten rid of his burro and gotten himself a new Cadillac.

He drinks coffee mixed with carrot juice. He figures since he's going to be up all night, he'd better be able to see in the dark.

∎

He's so wired with caffeine that he's noisy. His nerve endings vibrate so much they hum.

∎

This guy is always wired. He can't wear a hat anymore because it hurts his hair.

∎

This guy has so much caffeine in his system that he can't sleep alone anymore. He needs someone to help get his eyelids closed.

∎

The doctor told him he could have only one mug of coffee a day from now on. So he bought himself an inflatable wading pool and put a handle on it.

∎

He drinks so much coffee during the workday that he's dangerous when it's time to drive home. He generally gets there about 20 minutes before his car does.

∎

Some scientists now say that drinking coffee can help increase your sex activity. That's only fair. If it's going to keep you awake at night, the least it can do is give you something to do.

∎

Coffee will especially increase your sex life if you take it with a little bit of milk and two lumps of rhinoceros horns.

∎

But that's what the scientists claim; if a cup of coffee is the first thing you have in the morning, it could affect the last thing you have at night.

∎

The coffee manufacturers are capitalizing on this. One brand has already changed its name to "Maxwell House of Ill Repute."
One has changed its slogan to "Drink Yuban and You Can."
And, of course, you've heard the old saying: "Wham, bam, Sanka Ma'am."

We've had oat bran to lower our cholesterol; now we have coffee to lower our morals.

■

First scientists said coffee would increase your sex life, then they said it could increase the risk of heart attacks. I wish they'd make up their minds; I have to know how to dress.

■

After three or four cups of coffee you don't know whether you're going to meet your maker or three or four hookers.

■

Coffee's supposed to be good to the last drop. Now you find out you may be the last drop.

■

Of course, the price of coffee nowadays can give you a heart attack. You don't even have to drink it to get coffee nerves anymore; you just read the price of it at the supermarket.

■

Diners charge you now for a second cup of coffee, but they refill your ham and eggs for free.

■

Coffee is so expensive, you can double the value of a donut now by dunking it.

■

Some people used to keep their petty cash in a coffee can. Now they make out better if they just leave the coffee in there.

■

I don't know why the price of coffee is so high. Columbia must be trying to save up enough money to move to a better neighborhood.

A guy in my office used to have three cups of coffee every morning before starting work. Now he has two cups and calls his accountant to see if he can afford a third.

■

There's a guy at our office who drank 20 cups of coffee a day. He died last week, but he's still mingling in the company lounge.

■

He drinks so much coffee, he tosses and turns at his desk all day.

THE OFFICE BIGMOUTH

There are some people in an office who have absolutely nothing to say . . . but they always insist on saying it.

■

This one guy in our office has such a big mouth it takes four people to give him mouth-to-mouth resuscitation.

■

His mouth is moving so much it always comes out blurry in photographs.

■

His mouth is as close as we'll ever come in this life to a perpetual-motion machine.

■

We don't know if he makes sense when he talks or not. No one in the office has ever been dumb enough to listen to him.

■

It's a shame he wasn't on the *Titanic*. His hot air could have melted the iceberg.

■

There are three things that will never get together again: Martin & Lewis, China & Russia, and his upper and lower lips.

Have you ever seen those hot-air blowers that dry your hands in the restrooms? One of those was this guy's speech instructor.

■

A lot of people in our office say they'll never speak to him as long as they live. They don't want to interrupt.

■

He's actually a man of few words—but he keeps using them incessantly.

■

Abe Lincoln must have been talking about our office bigmouth when he said, "He can compress the most words into the smallest idea of any man I ever met."

■

The office bigmouth should remember, "A closed mouth gathers no feet."

UNLUCKY WORKER

One poor guy in our office is the unluckiest guy in the world. He bought a suit once that came with extra buttons in case he lost one. He lost a buttonhole.

■

We kid him. We say he's so unlucky, if it started raining soup he'd be stuck with nothing but a fork.

■

He was so unlucky that he once ruined his whole vacation. He slept every free minute . . . and dreamed he was at work.

. . . and the boss fired him.

. . . he's the only person I ever knew who got fired from his own dream.

. . . and you can't collect unemployment for that.

■

We all tried to convince this guy that he wasn't unlucky. He walked under a ladder once and absolutely nothing happened to him—until he came out the other side.

This guy was so unlucky, if a black cat walked in his path, the cat worried.

■

He considers 13 his unlucky number. And with good reason. That's how many times he's been hit by lightning.

■

This guy is so unlucky he has a black cloud over him wherever he goes. He has to hire a friend to get a suntan for him.

■

He's so unlucky, he carries a card that says, "In case of an accident, I'm not surprised."

■

He's such an unlucky worker, but he gives the company an honest day's work. Of course, it takes him a week to do it.

■

For the unlucky worker, success is not how high and how fast he reaches the top, but how high and fast he bounces back when he hits the bottom.

UNHAPPY CO-WORKER

I work with one guy who hates his work. He's always trying to invent get-rich schemes that will make him a million dollars so he can quit. Schemes like these:

Once he crossed a mink with a zebra. He got a beautiful pair of fur pajamas.

■

He even invented a coffee bean that makes you see double. If it keeps you awake all night, at least you have company.

■

This guy invented a combination shaving cream and plaster of paris. With that, men can shave and repair the dimple in their chin all at the same time.

He tried to develop a whiskey that was mixed with vitamins—for people who wanted to be high and mighty.

■

He had some success when he crossed a coffee bean with chili peppers. It tastes awful, but it stays hot.

■

Once he crossed an ordinary house mouse with a buffalo. We don't know what he got, but he had to sell the cat and buy an Indian.

■

He even crossed a thief with a pilot. The only trouble is, everytime he hits an airpocket he picks it.

■

He toyed with the idea of printing want ads on Kleenex tissue—for people who want a nose job.

■

He was enthused when he crossed an oyster with a woodpecker. He was trying to get pearls that already had a hole in them.

■

He crossed a mink with a seal and got a beautiful fur wet suit for wealthy skin divers.

■

Once he crossed a mink with a porcupine and got a fur coat that was relatively safe from pickpockets.

■

A woman emerged from a meeting and announced, "There is a feeling of togetherness in there. Everyone is reasonably unhappy."

Chapter 2

AT LARGE

THE KNOW-IT-ALL

It's easy to spot the know-it-all. He's the person who can often be wrong, but he's never in doubt.

▪

The know-it-all has done everything there is to be done . . . except shut up about it.

▪

The know-it-all has been everywhere. His major failing is that he keeps coming back.

▪

If the know-it-all doesn't know something, it's not worth knowing. Conversely, you can be sure if there's anything that's not worth knowing, he'll know it.

The know-it-all is generally well traveled. He's been told "shut your big fat face" in more than 40 different languages.

■

The know-it-all generally knows what he's talking about, but if he doesn't, it won't stop him.

■

One know-it-all in our office claimed he had a photographic mind. If he did, it was underdeveloped.

■

Know-it-alls don't get invited to many parties. They're about as much fun at a party as a frog in the punchbowl.

Inviting a know-it-all to a swinging party is like bringing a copy of *National Geographic* on your honeymoon.

■

You should always ask a know-it-all for his opinion . . . because you're going to get it anyway.

■

Bob Hudson set himself up as a hero for all know-it-alls when he said, "I haven't been wrong since 1961, when I thought I made a mistake."

■

He's living proof that stuffed shirts come in all sizes.

■

A young man started a new job and before long was telling everybody what they should do and how to do it. Finally, one of the older men who had been with the firm for a long time took the young man aside and said, "Son, you will have to show more patience with us. After all, we're not young enough to know everything."

THE BRAIN

We have a guy in our office who is very intelligent. He's all brains, which means that he has to sit down very carefully.

The man is brilliant. In the office, he actually tries to solve problems instead of just complaining about them.

■

He can find the solution to any problem . . . except what to do about all the dumb people who are working around him.

■

This guy actually sits at his desk and thinks. The rest of us have to use a computer.

■

This guy is so smart he doesn't even realize how dumb the rest of us are.

■

I think he's as smart as he is for a reason. Mother Nature didn't want to waste brains like that on a dumb person.

■

If I had an intellect like his I don't know what I'd do. Probably spend all my time trying to convince my friends that it was really me.

■

This man is brilliant. The only reason he has a body is so he can get his head from place to place.

■

I asked him once, "What's it like being a genius?" He said, "I'd tell you but you wouldn't understand."

■

This gentleman can sit at his desk and think for eight hours a day. I tried that once. I pulled a muscle in my ear.

■

The brain is the person who talks to himself because he likes dealing with intelligent people . . . and because no one else can understand him.

THE BORE

This friend of mine is so boring to be around that when he was a kid, he had at least three invisible playmates who never showed up again.
. . . they didn't want to be seen around him.

■

This guy I know is so dull that he has potato chip wounds all over his face. At parties, people keep mistaking him for the cheese dip.

■

This buddy of mine is so boring, he went to a wake once and the corpse kept yawning.

■

This guy I know is so boring he could put a cup of coffee to sleep.

■

This co-worker is such a boring conversationalist that the only way he can keep people awake when he talks to them is to gargle twice a day with No-Doz.

■

I knew a man who was so bland, if he wanted any flavor ice cream besides vanilla, he had to get a prescription from his doctor.

■

I worked with a guy who was so dull he had to have a pacemaker installed. Not only to keep his own heart beating, but also the hearts of people around him.

■

I knew a guy who was so boring he could never go to a party. Because once he walked in, it wasn't a party anymore.

■

This guy I knew was so boring, he made three-toed sloths look like party animals.

■

In every office, there's room for one bore.

What's the difference between a gossip and a bore? Talk about others and you're a gossip; talk about yourself and you're a bore.

THE SMOKER

The Attorney General's warning on cigarettes should say, "Smoking can be injurious to your health, and so can the people in the office who don't like your smoking."

■

Nonsmokers are really getting belligerent. One new office worker said, "Do you mind if I smoke?" His co-worker said, "Do you mind if I cut your nose off?"

■

One worker successfully sued for the right to work in a smoke-free environment—and he was a fireman.

■

My office had a great idea. Those who gave up smoking donated the money they would have spent on cigarettes to charity. We collected the money in a cigar box.

■

We have a cigar smoker in our office. I don't know what goes into his cigars, but I wish it would stay there.

■

This guy works the day shift, but his aromas hang around until about two in the morning.

■

This guy buys worse than cheap cigars. He buys cheap cigars, too, but only for special occasions.

■

I'll give you an idea how cheap his cigars are. The matches he uses to light them cost more.

■

Some of his cigars are so bad you can't even buy them. The store owner gives them away—to people who owe him money.

One guy I know smokes cigarettes made from wax crayons. They're just as bad for you, but the stains on your fingers are prettier.

∎

They say people who are trying to quit smoking substitute something else for it. It's true. Around our office, it's irritability.

∎

One office worker came up with this response when her colleague complained that her smoking made her sick.
"Well, then, if I were you, I'd give it up."

THE HYPOCHONDRIAC

I have a friend who is a chronic hypochondriac. Everytime science cures one disease, he invents a new one.

∎

This guy is such a chronic hypochondriac, he has to hire a team of doctors just to listen to his symptoms.

∎

So far he's had appendicitis, bronchitis, colitis . . . he also likes to get his symptoms in alphabetical order.

∎

This guy is an obsessive hypochondriac. He carries a copy of "Grey's Anatomy" around with him just in case a passerby happens to ask, "How are you?"

∎

This guy always knows there's something wrong with him. He visits his family doctor only to get a second opinion.

∎

A hypochondriac . . . that's someone who feels good only when he's not feeling good.

∎

Hypochondriacs like to get cured in a hurry . . . so they can get on to their next ailment.

The hypochondriac went to his doctor and the doctor said, "What's your problem today?" The hypochondriac said, "What've you got?"

▪

The hypochondriac went to the doctor and said, "Doc, I don't know what's wrong with me today." The doctor handed him a medical book and said, "Here. Pick something."

▪

Medicine is so expensive today that one hypochondriac I know finally wised up. He now only thinks he has ailments that are within his budget.

▪

It's easy to spot the office hypochondriac. He's the one who goes to the infirmary for monoaceticacidester of salicylicacid instead of aspirin.

▪

The hypochondriac is the one who gets acute laryngitis while everyone else has a cold.

THE ARGUER

We have a guy in our office who argues about everything. One day I said nothing to him and he disagreed with me.

▪

The man loves to debate. If you say "Hi" to this guy, you'd better be prepared to back it up.

▪

No matter what you say to this guy, he takes the other side. I think he was conceived while his parents were watching a televised election debate.

▪

This guy turns everything into an argument. Once I said "Nice day," and he said, "What makes you so sure?"

Once I showed him a picture of my children. Within a half hour he convinced me they weren't my kids.

■

A conversation with him is like a hockey game—sooner or later a fight is going to break out.

■

When this guy was married, his wife said "I do," and he said, "No, she doesn't."

■

I once saw this guy at a street corner where the traffic sign said "Walk," and this guy said, "Make me."

■

This guy could get on a bicycle built for two and argue about the seating arrangement.

■

He's a very confident arguer. He may be wrong, but he's never in doubt.

■

The office arguer doesn't have to worry about getting lost. There's always somebody who's willing to tell him where to go.

■

The arguer should remember John Gay's words: "Those who in quarrels interpose, must often wipe a bloody nose."

THE TRIVIA NUT

We have a trivia nut in our office. This guy has the knack for taking meaningless information and making it even more meaningless.

■

This guy has studied useless facts for so long he's become one.

■

He claims to know everything—except when to shut up.

This guy can tell you things you never knew, and after you know them you wish he hadn't told you.

■

This gentleman can explain little-known facts to you in such a way that you immediately understand why they were little known in the first place.

■

He's very versatile. He can make an ass of himself on any subject.

■

He'll tell you things whether you want to know them or not. He feeds you information pretty much the same way you have to give pills to a horse.

■

You can ask this guy anything. I've often asked him where the "off" switch was located on his voice box.

■

He devotes his life to knowing more and more about less and less. Pretty soon he'll know everything there is to know about absolutely nothing.

. . . but he'll still insist on telling you about it.

THE DRINKER

We have a guy in our office who drinks a little more than he should. He's due to retire in 12 years; his liver left 4 years ago.

■

This co-worker drinks so much he can't use a computer. His breath keeps melting the monitor screen.

■

This guy in our office drinks a bit. We always thought he had a beard, but it was just his breath running down his chin.

He claims drinking relieves his stress. It's also relieved him of his wife, his house, and three cars.

■

He claims if the Good Lord didn't want us to drink he wouldn't have made it easier to swallow than celery.

■

He orders the same thing for lunch every day: "Give me the two-martini businessman's special and hold the food."

■

The only time his eyes clear up is after the Red Cross Bloodmobile comes to the plant.

■

When the Red Cross Bloodmobile does come, most workers donate a pint. He donates a fifth.

■

He's a nice guy, though, so when quitting time comes, we wake him and tell him.

■

He has sworn off drink, though—at least three times today alone.

■

People who work with him have been forced to join AAA-AA. It's a group for people who are driven to drink.

■

There's a story of a worker whose boss was giving him a hard time concerning his conduct at a convention the previous night. The boss said, "I hear you were pushing a wheelbarrow down the street, singing at the top of your lungs. Now, what do you have to say for yourself?"

The employee answered, "I did, sir. Maybe I had a little too much to drink."

"That's no excuse," said the boss. "Look at the loss of prestige you may have brought on the whole company. What about that?"

"Yes, but I thought it didn't make much difference, since you ordered me to give you that ride in the wheelbarrow."

THE APPETITE

I have a friend who has a big appetite. He really likes his food
. . . and yours, too.

■

He enjoys three square meals a day . . . and four round ones.
. . . and a couple shaped like triangles, too.

■

This guy eats like there's no tomorrow. But just in case there
will be, he gets a doggie bag for it.

■

This guy has a very simple philosophy: He thinks the world
owes him a second helping of everything.

■

He's envious of fish because they have gills. They can eat and
breathe at the same time.

■

Talk about appetites, this guy could eat you out of house and
home and then ask, "What's for dessert?"

■

When this guy opened the refrigerator door, the only thing
in there that was safe was the little light bulb.

■

I took this girl on a dinner date. She said, "I guess I'll have the
steak and lobster." I said, "Guess again."

■

He's dangerous. Anyone who shares a lunch table with him
at the company cafeteria is required to wear a hard hat.

■

A lot of people bring their lunch to the office in a brown paper
bag. This guy I know uses a U-Haul trailer.

■

This friend of mine likes big servings. He's the only person I
know who orders his steaks with the hoofs still on.

What an appetite! This guy doesn't just clean his plate; he eats it.

■

This guy eats so fast, if you get near him when he's slurping his soup you could get caught up in the undertow.

THE SLOB

We have a guy in our office who is the sloppiest dresser in the world. He wears only Hart, Schaffner, and Hand-me-downs.

■

When he throws his old clothes in the Goodwill bin, it throws them back.

■

His clothes are worn so thin he could sit on a dime and tell whether it was heads or tails.
 . . . and also if F.D.R. had shaved that morning or not.

■

His shirts are all a disgrace. If it weren't for the frayed part, he'd have no collar at all.

■

He'd give you the shirt off his back—out of spite.
 . . . although, come to think of it, he's been wearing it so long, it probably doesn't come off his back.

■

This guy wears his clothes so long, they've been in style four times already.

■

He wears the sloppiest, oldest clothes in the world. I feel sorry for his poor wife. I don't know what she does for dust rags.

■

This guy is such a bad dresser, he doesn't need mothballs. Any moth who flies into his closet dies laughing.

He's so messy. Every day he has someone come in to mess up his desk.

FORGETFUL

I work with one of the most forgetful men in the world. Some days he calls in sick, then comes to work.

■

One year he made over $8,000 in overtime. He kept forgetting to go home.

■

He keeps asking for an extra two weeks' vacation because he forgets if he had any fun during the first two weeks.

■

He's very forgetful. Sometimes he calls customers, and when they say, "Hello," he says, "What do you want?"

■

The boss called him in and said, "Charlie, you have to do something about your memory." He said, "I agree. Who's Charlie?"

■

He's so forgetful. One doctor said, "There's nothing physically wrong with you." He left that doctor's office and immediately went out to get a first opinion.

■

His bad memory almost caused him to get a divorce until someone reminded him that he wasn't married.

■

He's very forgetful. He's the only guy I know who can successfully plan a surprise birthday party for himself.

■

He's so forgetful that he can't remember names. The only way he could get around that was to name his dog, "Dog."
    . . . and, still, every once in a while he calls the dog by saying, "Here, Kitty, Kitty."

He promised to take a senility test, but kept forgetting to show up.

■

He once figured out why he was so absent-minded, but forgot the answer.

THE DIMWIT

We have a guy in our office who is very slow-witted. The best way to make him laugh on a Friday is to tell him a joke on Wednesday.

■

His doctor once gave him a brain scan just by holding his head up to the light.

■

When he watches *Jeopardy*, the only thing he gets right is the channel.
. . . usually.

■

This guy spends a lot of time watching the "boob tube" . . . because he thinks it was named after him.

■

When this guy gets an idea, smoke comes out of his ears. That's because he has a wood-burning brain.

■

This fellow once locked his keys inside his car. It took him three and a half hours to get his family out.

■

Someone gave this guy a pair of cuff links once. He didn't have any shirts with French cuffs, so he had his wrists pierced.

He's so dumb he almost choked to death. He thought it was all right for him to eat red peppers because he's color blind.

■

I once tried to get this guy to go to night school and study "Spanish as a second language." He said he couldn't do it because he couldn't count that high.

■

They say the brain is the most mysterious organ in the human body. This gentleman hasn't figured out how his works yet.

■

His brain is unique. It begins to function the moment he awakes and doesn't stop until he gets to work.

■

The office dimwit is a lot like an elephant. He never forgets, but on the other hand, what does he have to remember?

THE CHEAPSKATE

We have a guy in our office who is so cheap he even tries to buy tattoos secondhand.

■

This guy has reached for fewer checks than Venus De Milo.

■

If you go to lunch with this guy Dutch treat, it means you pick up half the check and try to find some Dutchman who will pick up the other half.

■

This guy feels no remorse, no regrets. In fact, it's been 15 years since he's felt the inside of his own pockets.

■

This guy has a wallet that won't let dollar bills out of it. It's like a roach motel for money.

Everytime he takes a dollar out of his wallet, George Washington blinks at the light.

■

He can sometimes pass a dollar bill off as a five-dollar bill. He holds onto them so long that by the time he spends one, George Washington has grown a beard.

■

This fella can squeeze a nickel so tight that the buffalo on there actually undergoes a sex change.
... and I don't even want to talk about the poor Indian on the other side.

■

This gentleman always hopes that the airlines lose his luggage for a day or two. That way he doesn't have to tip the bellhop.

■

He's so cheap it reminds me of the little boy whose teacher asked him, "If you had five apples and I asked for one, how many would you have left?"
And he answered, "Five."

■

She's so cheap she puts slugs in her penny loafers.

■

Martha Raye once learned a valuable lesson about being cheap while dining at Jimmy Durante's table. A waiter passed by with a serving of shishkebob all aflame. Miss Raye was startled and exclaimed, "What on earth was that?" Durante explained, "A customer who only left a $10 tip."

■

When it comes to giving, he stops at nothing.

Part Two

POWER

"A friend in power
is a friend lost."

Henry Adams

Chapter 3

At WORK

"THEY"

"They" are always in charge. We never know who "They" are. All we know is that "They" are never as smart as "Us."

■

It's unfair. "They" make all the business decisions. But when those decisions are wrong, "We" get laid off.

■

We're never sure exactly who "They" are. But "They" get better parking spaces than "We" do.

■

"They" are like the boogieman. For characters who don't really exist, they sure can cause "Us" a lot of sleepless nights.

How did "They" get to be so powerful? "We" let them.
"They" are absolutely necessary. If "They" weren't there,
"We" would be responsible for the mess we're in.

■

Why do we refer to them as "They"? Because someone's got
this world into a mess, and it certainly couldn't be "Us."

■

"They" generally are mean, greedy, and heartless. Why?
Because "They" have the power that "We" would like to have.

■

It's sobering to think that if there were no "They," then "We"
would be "Them."

■

It's easier to go through life blaming someone else. That's
why "They" get the blame for what "We" should be doing.

■

"They" are the ones who come in late, leave early, and in
between drive everyone else crazy.

■

"They" are the ones, when you say "Good morning" answer
"Thank you."

■

"They" share Samuel Goldwyn's philosophy: "I am not always right—but I am never wrong."

THE BOSS

Some people are leaders and some people are followers. And
then some people are like the boss—they just sit there.

■

It takes only a minimum of intelligence to be boss. Most of
them are well qualified.

Cream always rises to the top. But in many cases, it curdles before it gets there.

■

Some people have the uncanny ability to walk into an empty room and immediately become the underling.

■

My boss always says to me: "I want it done today. If I wanted it done tomorrow, I would have given it to you tomorrow." Then I learned to say back to him: "I can't have it done until tomorrow. If I'd known you wanted it today, I would have worked on it all day yesterday."

■

My boss rules his workers with an iron fist. Unfortunately, he makes all his plans with a wooden head.

■

During one pep talk, my boss said, "In this office, I am the shepherd and you are my flock." So all the workers said, "Baaa."

■

My boss said to me: "I'm the boss because I'm a natural leader, and you're a natural disaster."

■

My boss doesn't get along with anyone. If he were an island, he'd fight with the water.

■

My boss has the personality of a piranha who woke up on the wrong side of the river.

■

The definition of a boss is someone who, when you get to work early, comes in late, and when you are late, comes in early.

■

Some people like to compare their boss to a diaper . . . full of _____ and all over their behinds.

SECRETARIES

Secretaries have a lot of authority in executive offices. Yessir, they have the power of the hold button.

■

Secretaries have those four little words that can bring the entire corporate world to a halt: "He's in a meeting."

■

When you boil it down to the basics, a secretary is nothing more than a baby-sitter for an executive.

■

You show me a secretary who insists that her boss make his own coffee, and I'll show you a secretary who drinks tea.

■

One boss said to his secretary, "What does my appointment book show for today?" She said, "It shows a big stain. I spilled the coffee you made me make this morning all over it."

■

One boss said to his secretary, "I'd like a cup of coffee, please." The secretary said, "I'd like a 23 percent salary increase. Looks like we're both out of luck."

■

Without secretaries, executives would starve to death. There's not a one of them who can make his own lunch arrangements.

■

My secretary finally cured me of asking her to shop for little gifts for my wife. Last Valentine's Day, she bought her a red Porsche.

■

My secretary used to constantly get offended when I would say things like: "Call my girl." I finally had to say to him, "Look, Herman . . ."

■

One secretary called another to see if they might get together for lunch. The problem was could they both get off work at the same time. One said, "Look, why don't you have my boy call your boy."

Why is it that a generally bright businessman will ignore his secretary's advice and pay a consultant $200 an hour for the same thing?

RECEPTIONISTS

Receptionists are tough to get past. They're the middle linebackers of the corporate world.

■

Everyone must go through the receptionist. They are to the office what metal detectors are to the airport.

■

One receptionist was so tough, when she'd say, "Whom would you like to see?" I'd say, "Anyone but you."

■

Receptionists are the first people salespeople meet when they make a cold call. And if the receptionists are doing a good job, they're the only person salespeople meet when they make a cold call.

■

Receptionists greet you when you walk into an office, but they also keep you in the waiting room. They're a cross between a welcome mat and a pit of quicksand.

■

Receptionists make sure that you stay in the waiting room until called. They are a live "hold" button.

■

The receptionist said, "Would you like a cup of coffee?" I said, "Yes, I would." She said, "Me too, but I'm not allowed to leave my desk."

■

I said, "I'd like to see Mr. Wilson."
The receptionist said, "Have a seat, please."
I said, "Do you know what I'm here for?"
She said, "I'd say about an hour and a half."

Receptionists show little concern for your priorities or your schedule when you visit their offices. They are answering machines incarnate.

■

But receptionists are always considerate. If you can't wait, they say, "Just leave your name and number and I'll forget about them the minute you leave."

■

Chess is a game in which people sit for hours, staring ahead, not moving a muscle. We have the same thing in our office. It's called a receptionist.

■

On Wednesday a salesperson walked up to the receptionist and asked to see her boss. She quickly responded that he was away for the weekend. The salesperson replied, "Last weekend or this weekend?"

Chapter 4

AWAY FROM WORK

THE POWER GAME OF GOLF

Golf is a lesson in humility rolled up into a little white ball.

■

I find that a golf hole is the longest distance between two points.

■

Golf is a combination of fun, excitement, exercise, competition . . . everything but skill.

■

Golf is misery with a caddy.

■

Golf is not a game; it's punishment for not taking up another sport.

A bad round of golf breaks your heart more than a broken romance. Generally you're not betting on a romance.

■

Golf is a very tough game. Just when you think you know how to play it, somebody gives you a starting time.

■

Golf is a game you can play all your life . . . and enjoy maybe three days in that time.

■

Golf is a game of beautiful fairways, lovely ponds, gorgeous trees . . . and ugly swings.

■

Golf is a frustrating game. It's amazing how you can destroy a beautiful woodland setting by putting a tiny hole in the middle of it.

■

Golf is a difficult game. It's the only sport I know that ends with a round of drinks in the clubhouse.

■

Men don't give birth. They don't have to. They get all the pain they need from golf.

■

Golf is a great weekend sport. It makes going back to work on Monday seem almost a relief.

■

Golf is nature's way of telling you: "This is what life looks like from behind a tree."

■

Golf is a very powerful game. It's the only sport that can convert a duck pond into a water hazard.

■

Golf is a pretty game, though. You can smell the freshly mowed grass and the pine trees. When I play, you can smell a few other things, too.

The way I've been playing lately, golf is a series of out of bounds markers with a golf course attached.

■

You know why they call them "greens fees"? Because most golfers very rarely use the fairways.

■

I consider my golf clubs a kitchen appliance. With them I can slice anything.

■

I've had some bad things happen to me on the golf course. They usually happen right after my back swing.

■

My golf ball has never met a water hazard it didn't like.

■

Bowling has one advantage over golf. You very rarely lose a ball.

■

Golf is nature's way of making everyone a comedian.

■

People say, "If you're playing golf for fun, why do you keep score?" That's so you can have a scorecard to show the guys in the clubhouse what you've been cursing at all afternoon.

■

Playing golf for fun is like going to the dentist because you enjoy rinsing.

■

Anybody who plays golf for fun either has a good swing or some bad information.

■

Whoever said golf was fun either has never played golf or has never had any fun.

■

Sex is more fun than golf, it's easier than golf, and it's less expensive than golf . . . except you don't get to ride in a cart.
. . . and it's usually harder to get a starting time.

I play golf every chance I get. I think the world needs more laughter.

Lawyers

We have more lawyers in America now than we have smog—only the smog doesn't charge $225 an hour.

■

Everybody in America now is either a lawyer or somebody who needs one.

■

There are two big professions in America now—doctors and lawyers. John Wayne wiped out all the Indian chiefs.

■

One kid graduated from law school and immediately sued his parents . . . for making him go to law school.

■

There are a lot of divorce lawyers in our country now. This nation's second-highest-paid profession is alimony.
. . . The first-highest-paid profession is divorce lawyer.

■

When you buy a girl a drink, the bartender automatically brings a martini and a prenuptial agreement.

■

Those are the two major pastimes in America today—acquiring worldly goods and dividing them equally.

■

Divorce is not as prevalent in America as you might think—only among married people.

Nowadays we even have Jacoby & Meyers that operates in the corner of a department store. You can take your entire settlement out in house and garden tools.

I don't think I'd use a lawyer who works in a department store. That's like going to Jack in the Box to have your appendix removed.

■

When you live in the land of fruits and nuts, you have to have a lot of lawyers to keep them separated.

■

When a California lawyer hangs out his shingle, it's made out of his old surfboard.

■

A client was angry at his lawyer for charging him for advice that the lawyer simply looked up in a book. The client figured he could have bought the book, found his own answer, and saved lots of money. He mentioned his protests to the lawyer, who calmly responded, "You pay me, not for owning the book, but for knowing what page to look on."

■

Only a lawyer could write documents with more than ten thousand words and call them briefs.

TRAFFIC COPS

Traffic cops probably have more power than anyone in the world, with the possible exception of mothers-in-law.

■

Police officers look imposing. They have more things hanging from their belt than I have hanging in my closet.

Traffic cops are necessary, though. They're the only thing that some people obey while they're driving.

■

You should always be polite to traffic officers. You should be polite to anyone who has handcuffs, a gun, a billy club, and the power of the state on his side.

■

Motorcycle patrolmen always look imposing. It's the boots, the uniform, and the dark glasses that do it. Of course, the fact that some of them are 6'3" and weigh 240 pounds helps a little bit, too.

■

There's only one thing worse than seeing a flashing red light in your rear-view mirror. That is not seeing it and backing into it.

■

Police should warn us when they're hiding along the highway. They should give us at least three or four miles to allow us to slow down to the speed limit.

■

A police officer stopped me on the highway for speeding. He said, "What's the rush?" I said, "It's for safety reasons, Officer. I want to get home before all the accidents happen."

■

The police officer stopped a man for driving under the influence. He looked at his driver's license and said, "How much do you weigh?" The man said, "One-eighty-six and a fifth."

■

There are rare instances where some towns allow their officers to misuse their authority. Like this one small town where I got a ticket for having my windshield wipers going the wrong way on a one-way street.

■

A patrol car began chasing an elderly female driver who was speeding along the highway. The chase continued so long that another patrol car joined, and then a third. The woman kept gaining speed and finally pulled into a gas station. She stopped the car and began running into the ladies room. When she came out the officers were waiting for her. She said, "I'll bet for awhile there you boys didn't think I was going to make it, did you?"

■

A patrol officer stopped a car that was going the wrong way on a one-way street. He said to the driver, "Where do you think you're going?" The driver said, "I don't know, but I must be late. Everyone else is going home."

■

A police officer stopped a car for going through a stop sign. The driver said, "Yes, but I did slow down."
The officer said, "You're supposed to stop."
The driver said, "I did slow down, though."
The police officer said, "The sign said to stop."
The man said, "But I did slow down."
The officer said, "You're required to stop."
The driver said, "Stop, slow down, what's the difference?"
The officer pulled him out of the car and started whacking him on the head with his nightstick.
The man said, "Hey. You're hurting my head."
The officer said, "Right. Do you want me to stop or slow down?"

■

Sometimes cops aren't as helpful as they like to think. Like the judge who asked the litigants if they could have settled this matter out of court. The defendant answered, "That's what we were doing, Your Honor, when a couple of cops butted in."

SECURITY OFFICERS AT THE AIRPORT

Security people at the airport have a tremendous amount of power. They're the only ones who can make you empty your pockets immediately besides a spouse or an IRS investigator.

■

Some of these security people are very dedicated. Instead of saying, "Welcome aboard," they say, "Who goes there ... friend or foe?"

If they're going to frisk me, I don't care if they have a cold personality. I just want them to have warm hands.

■

Some of these airport security people are very dedicated. Last week I was in a boarding area and all the passengers were planning a break.

■

There are three ways to travel now . . . tourist, first class, and suspect.

■

They frisk everybody very thoroughly. It's not too much of a delay . . . unless you happen to get in line behind Roseanne Arnold.

■

I was on one flight where they really frisked everyone very thoroughly. For the first hour of the flight, everyone in the piano lounge sang like Wayne Newton.

■

Those airline searches are so thorough, it's costing me money. I've had to move up to a more expensive brand of underwear.

■

One airline security guard searched me so thoroughly, we still write.

■

I remember once they stripped me, searched the lining of my clothes, and took the heels and soles off my shoes looking for things . . . oh no, wait . . . that wasn't the airline security people, it was the IRS.

■

One airline security guard was so tough he strip-searched everyone. I didn't mind so much, but the pilot was furious.

■

I don't mind tough security. I always volunteer to be frisked, but the stewardesses keep refusing.

Some of them are very thorough. I bought insurance last week, and the search at the airport also qualified as my physical.

■

One security guard frisked me in places where I would never keep a bomb even if I had one.

■

Bob Hope says he was once searched by a guy with cold hands. He landed in Chicago 45 minutes before his plane did. Hope says, "Just tell me what you're looking for and I'll tell you where I keep it."

■

We should be careful about whom we flex our muscles with. It reminds me of the airline passenger who was giving the luggage checker a hard time. Another passenger waiting in line observed the treatment the young man was enduring. When his turn finally came, the man commented that this must be a thankless job, especially having to put up with jerks like the previous customer.

The checker responded, "Oh, it's all right, I've already gotten even with him."

"What do you mean?" asked the man.

"Well, he's all set to go to Philadelphia," said the young man. "But his luggage is on its way to San Francisco."

FLIGHT ATTENDANTS

Flight attendants have a lot of power. If you don't do what they want, they can deprive you of your food. And if you really misbehave, they can bring you your food and make you eat it.

■

Flight attendants are there primarily for our safety. That's good, because if anything goes wrong, that seat-bottom flotation device ain't going to do you a helluva lot of good.

■

Flight attendants wield a lot of power. Name anyone else who can force you to bring your seat backs to a fully upright and locked position.

The airlines hire only people with strong character to be flight attendants. It takes a lot of intestinal fortitude to serve some of that airline food.

. . . and even more courage to do it with a smile.

■

And flight attendants get asked some stupid questions, too. One traveler asked, "If the world came to an end while we were up here, would we crash?" The flight attendant said, "Where?"

■

Flight attendants are usually bright and cheery. That's because they don't *have to* eat the airline food.

■

Flight attendants have to be sure, too, that all carry-on luggage must fit under the seat in front of you, in the overhead bin, or at least on the plane in general.

Some people carry on so much baggage, you're not sure whether they're flying to Oakland or about to climb the south face of Mt. Everest.

Some people carry so much luggage on board that when they land, instead of calling for a SkyCap, they call for a Bekins Moving Van.

HOSPITAL ADMISSION CLERKS

The toughest thing to get past is not the Washington Redskins defensive line. It's a clerk in a hospital-admission office when you don't have the proper insurance forms.

■

Au revoir means good-bye. *Arrividerci* means good-bye. *Sayonara* means good-bye. So does telling a hospital admissions clerk that you don't have any insurance coverage.

■

In a war, all you have to give is your name, rank, and serial number. In a hospital, though, you also have to give your insurance carrier.

To a hospital admissions clerk only one thing is incurable—
not having insurance.

■

Hospital admissions clerks all say the same two things first:
"Have a seat, please" and "How do you intend to pay for this?"
If you answer the second one wrong, you have to give the seat
back.

■

Sometimes patients get so angry they want to beat up the
admissions clerk, which is all right. They already have insurance.

■

Going into a hospital is difficult. If there's nothing seriously
wrong with you when you get there, there will be by the time you
get done dealing with the admissions clerk.

■

Hospital admissions clerks are mean. They're the only people
who would say "Have a seat, please" to a hemorrhoid patient.
It's even more ironic when they tell the same patient: "You
have to pay up front."

MAITRE D'S

Maitre d's are powerful. They control the seating arrangement of the world.

■

Maitre d's always expect a tip. If they were leading you to the
electric chair, they'd have their palm out.

■

The average maitre d' is 10 percent haughty and 90 percent
open palm.

■

Maitre d's expect a tip just for showing you to your seat. I
would gladly tell most of them where to go for nothing.

The tip for the maitre d' generally cost as much as your first drink . . . and you can't nurse a maitre d' for most of the night.

■

The best way to find out where the worst seat in any restaurant is, is to show the maitre d' a dollar bill and ask him if he has change for it.

■

I once went to an elegant restaurant, held up a dollar bill to the maitre d', and said, "Can you get us a nice table?" He said, "I'm sorry, sir, but we don't serve food to go."

■

Maitre d's make money just for allowing you to sit down in their establishment. When you analyze it, they're not much better than coin-operated toilets.

■

Maitre d's are anatomically interesting. Even if you're taller than they are, they can still look down their noses at you.

■

I had to tip one maitre d' so much for a nice table, that when I left, I took the table with me.

■

Maitre d's are often called upon to handle very delicate situations. Once, while George Bernard Shaw was dining in a restaurant, an orchestra began to play rather loudly. The music continued for some time. Finally Shaw called the maitre d' over and asked if the orchestra took requests.

The maitre d' exclaimed that they did and asked what Mr. Shaw would like them to play.

"Ask them to play dominoes until I have finished eating," he replied.

WAITERS

Waiters can sometimes be like children. It seems as though they can take nine months to arrive.

"Waiter" seems to be a misnomer. They are "servers"; we're the ones who do the waiting.

■

The waiter's motto seems to be: If you need anything just call me . . . then call me again . . . and again . . . and again.

■

The term "gratuity" seems to be especially applicable to most waiters. It means "something for nothing."

■

Being a waiter means playing a game with the customer—I'll get your soup, if you can get my attention.

■

All things come to those who wait . . . except hot soup.

■

I had one waiter who was so slow, by the time he brought the hot chili peppers they were lukewarm chili peppers.

■

When I paid my restaurant check, I had to leave 15 percent for the waiter and 6 percent for the state, and neither one of them did a thing for me during the meal.

■

My waiter wanted an 18 percent tip, plus 2 percent for pain and suffering. He burnt his thumb while carrying my soup.

■

The waiter asked if I could leave the tip in cash. I asked why. He said the owner of the restaurant was even slower than he was.

■

A customer complains to the slow waiter that his service was miserable. The waiter said, "How do you know? You haven't had any yet."

■

In most restaurants today, you find that the food is frozen and the waiters are fresh.

PARKING ATTENDANTS

Parking attendants are always easy to spot. They usually wear a bright-red vest and a lead foot.

■

You know what valet parking is . . . that's being a demolition derby driver for tips only.

■

We have a lot of faith in parking attendants. We give them a $38,000 vehicle and they give us a cardboard tag with a number on it.

■

One parking attendant drove my car so wildly that when he brought it back, it had its tailpipe between its legs.

■

I don't trust parking attendants. When they take my car I always check the mileage, and when they bring it back, I always count the tires.

■

I told one parking attendant that I didn't want my car being used for joy rides. He said, "Oh, I can't take it off the lot, sir. I don't have a driver's license."

■

All parking attendants drive like maniacs. I think most of them are former test pilots who are down on their luck.

■

One parking attendant drove my car away so fast that the tires squealed, and so did I.

■

These guys are the craziest drivers in the world and we leave our cars with them. It's like asking a family of coyotes to mind your cat while you're away.

■

We usually tip parking attendants fairly well. Not because they do such a superb job; we're just so glad to see our cars again.

Part Three

POLITICS

"Being in politics is like being
a football coach. You have to
be smart enough to understand
the game and stupid enough to
think it's important."

Eugene McCarthy

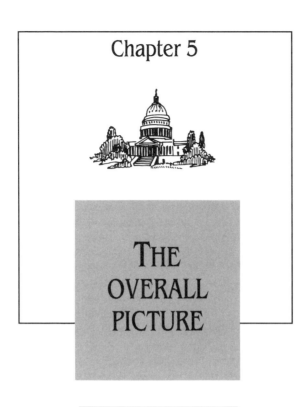

Chapter 5

THE OVERALL PICTURE

WASHINGTON, DC

I like to come to Washington, DC, every once in awhile . . . and visit with my money.

■

I feel very much at home in Washington, DC. After April 15th, I feel like one of the owners.

■

Washington, DC, is the last place our money stops before going overseas.

■

The parks and trees are beautiful in Washington, DC. Well, look at all the fertilizer they get.

Washington, DC, serves a very important function in our system of government. It keeps all of our politicians in one place where it's easier to keep an eye on them.

Washington, DC, is where we send our elected officials. It's like a summer camp for politicians.

It's a lot like a summer camp. This is where politicians come and learn to sink or swim.

■

Washington, DC, is the home of 90 percent of the laws in our country, and 100 percent of the comedy.

■

Washington, DC, lately has become a city where it's not so much "who you know," but "what do you know and when did you know it?"

■

If so many intelligent people are elected to be sent to Washington, why do they call it the *seat* of our government?

■

How prophetic L'Enfant was when he laid out Washington as a city that goes around in circles.

—John Mason Brown

■

Traffic is getting so bad in Washington, DC. The only way to change lanes is to trade cars.

THE GOVERNMENT

Governments are absolutely essential. Without them, we'd never know which anthem to sing before ball games.

■

Government is necessary to maintain order. If it weren't for government, the entire world would look like a rock concert.

. . . except not as noisy.

There are different forms of government. There is a dictatorship where one person rules the country. Then there's democracy where you have to be elected to office before becoming a dictator.

■

Government is common sense run aground.

■

Government is rules that control the people, usually written by politicians who don't want to hang around with the people.

■

There is nothing wrong with government that couldn't be cured by getting rid of the politicians.

■

Thomas Jefferson said, "The best government is no government at all." Lately it seems that's what we get closer and closer to electing.

■

Government seems to be able to come up with solutions that are more troublesome than the problem.

■

We live in a land where majority rules, but the politicians and the press seem to decide who the majority will be.

■

The purpose of government is to establish rules and maintain order . . . sort of like referees at a professional wrestling match.

■

Practically anyone can serve in our government, but you have to be dead a goodly number of years before you can get your picture on a stamp.
Does the Post Office know something we don't?

■

I don't make jokes. I just watch the government and report the facts.

—Will Rogers

POLITICS

You can't get blood from a rock, but that never stops the politicians from passing bills that keep on trying.

■

We're finding out a lot of our politicians do nothing but it costs us a lot for them to do it.

■

Politicians can be tough. They want everything done right . . . unless they're doing it

■

Don't you get a kick out of politicians who hate the filthy rich? Rich people spend their own money.

■

All politicians should stay physically fit. In case they ever have to work for a living.

■

I think most Americans are willing to pay their fair share. And we know most politicians are ready to collect it.

■

That's the trouble with politicians—they get to vote on their raises instead of earning them.

■

Some politicians elect to just do nothing after they leave office. They've had so much practice at it.

■

Even as a kid everyone knew he'd go into politics. Each time his father gave him his allowance, he'd call him in for an audit.
. . . He would never come in for dinner. He was always out back straddling a fence.

■

Politics is fun. They get involved in name calling, mud slinging, and back stabbing, just so they can earn the right to be called "The Honorable."

If politicians want to give themselves a raise, they should get a job first.

■

We have only two types of politicians nowadays . . . those who are running for President and those who are being investigated.

■

Politics is getting pretty nasty, isn't it. They're starting to make professional wrestling look honest.

■

They're getting pretty vicious in politics nowadays. The oath of office ends with a denial of all the charges.

■

The new policy in America is innocent until elected to office.

■

You can call a politician a conservative or you can call him a liberal. The only thing they really resent being called is a politician.

■

We'll have politics with us for the rest of all time. It's going to take us that long to pay off the debts they've run up.

■

Politician: Someone who divides his time between running for office and running for cover.

■

A lawyer spoke up and said, "Mine is obviously the oldest profession. It dates back to before the Garden of Eden. Surely you can recognize in the serpent the voice of an attorney.

A doctor quickly disputed him. "Before that, you remember, the Lord had to form a woman out of Adam's rib. That surely took medical knowledge."

An engineer took up the challenge. "If you remember, before Adam and Eve, the Lord God said, 'Let there be light.' Surely that was a sign of engineering capability."

Then a politician spoke up. "I'm afraid that all of you gentlemen are not completely aware of our antecedents. The politician, I am certain, was clearly first. You may remember the first words of the Bible: 'In the beginning, there was chaos.' and who else but a politician could have created THAT?"

———————————■———————————

All of our greatest comedians have had something to say about politics, like the following:

There's nothing wrong with our foreign policy that faith, hope, and clarity couldn't cure.

—Henny Youngman

If we're lucky, the Russians will steal some of our secrets, and then they'll be two years behind us.

—Mort Sahl

With politicians horning in, our comedian business is over-crowded.

—Will Rogers

This country is not prosperous. It's just got good credit.

—Will Rogers

The Congressional Record, a dictionary and a political platform are the three least-used things in existence today.

—Will Rogers

You know what the Pentagon is? That's a big building in Washington that has five sides—on almost every issue.

—Henny Youngman

The reason there are so few women politicians is that it is too much trouble to put make-up on two faces.

—Maureen Murphy

Political baby-kissing must come to an end—unless the size and age of the babies are materially increased.

—W. C. Fields

Chapter 6

THE
PEOPLE
OF
GOVERNMENT

PRESIDENTS

Presidents are just like the rest of us. They don't report their golf winnings to the IRS either.

■

The presidency is more than money. Most people would give anything to out-rank the IRS for four years.

■

When you get elected President, you get your own valet. Some people call him the Vice-President.

■

Being President is a unique job. Only 41 people have held that job and they stay for only a brief period. It's like marrying Zsa Zsa Gabor.

Grover Cleveland was our 22nd and 24th President. He got 4 years off in the middle there for good behavior.

■

Harry Truman once said, "The White House is the finest prison in the world." If he felt that way, why did he run for resentencing?

■

Truman used to say exactly what he was thinking, which was so unusual for a politician . . . to be thinking.

■

We've had some silly quotes from Presidents too. George Washington said, "I cannot tell a lie." He didn't have to. They didn't have tax returns back then.

■

Franklin Delano Roosevelt said, "The only thing we have to fear is fear itself." But he never played golf with Gerry Ford.

■

FDR was our only President elected to four terms. Back in those days, Rich Little would have had to learn only one voice.

■

Lyndon Johnson said, "When the President of the United States speaks, the world listens," and the dog that he used to pick up by the ears said, "What?"

■

Henry Clay said, "I'd rather be right than President." Ronald Reagan came along and proved it didn't have to be a choice.

■

George Will said, "Ronald Reagan has held the two most demeaning jobs in the country—President of the United States and radio broadcaster for the Chicago Cubs."

■

Eisenhower found golf very relaxing. That's understandable. Only someone who had been through WWII would find golf relaxing.

Kennedy played touch football instead of golf. He preferred contact sports. Golf didn't become a contact sport until Gerry Ford started to play it.

■

Nixon opened his presidential library. It's been open only one day and already 18½ books are missing.

■

Ronald Reagan has a library too. He just can't remember where.

■

They haven't picked the site of George Bush's presidential library yet. It'll probably be on a converted broccoli farm.
. . . he'll do anything to stop that stuff from growing.

■

Ronald Reagan was an actor in Hollywood before becoming President. The others didn't learn that skill until after they took office.

■

Each of the Presidents brought something different to the White House. The Nixons introduced some new furniture, the Reagans brought new dishes, Bush some new paintings, and the Fords added a lot of new divots to the lawn.

■

You can always spot Gerry Ford's Secret Service guys. They're the ones carrying first-aid kits.

■

When there's hostilities in the world, George Bush plays golf for relaxation. Gerry Ford used to do it as an offensive measure.

■

President Ford was one of the few people to get the job without first having to have his name on a bumper sticker.

■

Reagan settled all disputes. He listened to both sides, woke up, and gave his decision.

George Bush travels so much. I don't know why. Air Force One doesn't have a frequent-flyer bonus program.

■

George Bush vacations through each crisis. Ronald Reagan used to sleep through his.

■

George Bush is energetic and fast; he likes to move around. I got an idea! Why don't we let him deliver the mail?

———————■———————

Did you read what this writer dug up in George Washington's diary? I was so ashamed I sat up all night reading it.

—Will Rogers

Once a friend bet Will Rogers that he couldn't make President Coolidge laugh. But Will won. When he was introduced to Coolidge, he said, "Beg pardon, I didn't catch the name."

—Will Rogers

John F. Kennedy's father gave him a choice: You can either run for President—or go to camp.

—Bob Hope

They were going to put out a Nixon stamp, but they stopped; people were spitting on the wrong side.

—Henny Youngman

When I was a boy I was told that anybody could become President; I'm beginning to believe it.

—Clarence Darrow

In America, anyone can become President. That's one of the risks you take.

—Adlai Stevenson

VICE-PRESIDENTS

Expectant fathers are like Vice-Presidents . . . they put you in a room someplace and forget about you.

■

While they're in office, Vice Presidents are seen slightly less often than Elvis Presley.

■

Let's face it, when the President's healthy we need a Vice President about as much as Robin Williams needs a straight man.

■

To be President of the United States, you have to be over 35 and a citizen of the United States. To be Vice-President, you have to be over 35, a citizen of the United States, and have a sense of humor.

■

The office of Vice-President has never commanded much respect. When our founding fathers invented that office they thought it would go to a Tory.

■

The Vice-President is always out of place. You feel like a pair of brown shoes in a tuxedo rental shop.

■

Andy Warhol said that everyone in the world is famous for 15 minutes. But you forfeit that right if you get elected Vice President of the United States.

■

Vice-President is the only position of exile that a person is elected to.

■

You've heard of the office of Vice President—that's Washington's version of "The Invisible Man."

■

Vice President is a strange job. It means when the President has nothing to do, you have even less.

When the President arrives the band plays "Hail to the Chief." When the Vice President arrives the band takes their break.

■

The Vice President doesn't need a big car. Anytime he has to go anywhere officially the car is usually provided by the funeral director.

■

Being Vice President is not the most visible job in the world. It's like being a pinch hitter for Reggie Jackson.

■

Vice President is a thankless job. When you take the oath of office, you feel as if you should place your hand on a paperback Bible.

■

They know it's not a very visible job when they administer the oath of office. They say, "Raise your right hand and repeat after me . . . I, don't bother to state your name . . ."

■

A good Vice-President should be seen and not heard . . . once he's heard, he's usually never seen again.

■

Will Rogers felt the Vice-President had the easiest job in the country. "All he has to do is get up every morning and say, 'How's the President?'"

■

When a Vice-President runs, he goes from Vice-President to either President or private citizen. Either one is a step up.

———————————■———————————

Congress kinda got the Vice-President going now. He sits up there with a hammer, but none of them are close enough that he can really do much good with it. It's a terrible job and why they ever wished it on as important a person as the Vice-President . . .

—Will Rogers

A vice president is a bit of executive fungus that forms on a desk that has been exposed to a conference.

—Fred Allen

CONGRESS AND SENATE

It's hard for Congress to figure out how to spend money. For so many years they've just been giving it away.

∎

They tried to save money by shutting down the parks and monuments. Maybe if they just shut down Congress for a few days the problem would solve itself.

∎

Congress and the President fight every year over the budget. But there's never any suspense over who's going to lose . . . us.

∎

Congress has more trouble organizing their budget each year than the rest of us . . . and they don't even have to pay taxes on theirs.

∎

It's typical government logic . . . they spend a fortune each year trying to cut spending.

∎

Congress keeps spending money they don't have . . . it wouldn't be so bad if they let us pay our taxes that way too.

∎

Congress voted themselves a 33⅓ percent raise. That's a hefty pay raise for unskilled labor.

∎

I love Congress. It takes them 7 volumes and 26,000 pages to explain how they simplified something.

Congress voted themselves a hefty salary increase. But it's still cheaper than buying our Congressmen from defense contractors.

■

Many people feel Congress is like the young man who went to a psychiatrist. The doctor listened to the man and then offered his insight: "It appears to me you have trouble making decisions. Would you agree?" The young man thought about it a moment and replied, "Well, yes and no."

■

Jay Leno made this remark about our senator's job performance: "I saw a senator on one of those Sunday morning talk shows the other day and he said that the actions of the Senate have created a lot of jobs for a lot of citizens.

Yeah, but, let's face it, you can't make a career out of jury duty."

■

Congress could be compared to a sausage . . . a mixture of pleasant and not so pleasant things.

———————————■———————————

Congress just killed the Aid to Education Bill. If there's one thing those fellas have to worry about, it's educated voters.

—Robert Orben

Legislatures are . . . like animals in the zoo. You can't do anything about 'em. All you can do is just stand and watch 'em.

—Will Rogers

Our Senate always opens with a prayer, followed by an investigation.

—Will Rogers

Reader, suppose you are an idiot. And suppose you were a member of Congress. But, I repeat myself.

—Mark Twain

Senator: Person who makes laws in Washington when not doing time.

—Mark Twain

Congress is so strange. A man gets up to speak and says nothing . . . nobody listens . . . and then they all disagree.

—Will Rogers

THE SUPREME COURT

Imagine our constitutional questions being decided by only nine people. That's like entrusting our way of life to the Judds, The Bee Gees, and The New Kids on the Block.

■

Some people in this country don't even know what the Supreme Court is. They think it's where Diana Ross and her friends play basketball.

■

The Supreme Court decides what's right or wrong in this nation. That's funny. It takes nine people to do what Alex Trebek does all by himself on *Jeopardy*.

■

The Supreme Court is the final judge in any disagreements. They're like the mother-in-law in a family argument.

■

There is no appeal from the Supreme Court. If you lose there, you finally have to pay your attorney.

■

Our Supreme Court has been going conservative. They ordered new robes and they all came back with two right sleeves.

■

Our Supreme Court has gone so conservative. They took a group portrait the other day, and the Court had moved so far right only four of the judges were still in the picture.

The Supreme Court was liberal for a long time. It got so you had to commit a crime to get any rights in this country.

■

Opponents argue that a conservative Supreme Court could send us back to the days when criminals were considered second-class citizens.

■

Proponents say it could mark a return to law and order in this country. You remember law and order—that's what we used to have before the lawyers got involved.

■

There is an old story that someone had told Lord Salisbury that a bishop was greater than a judge, for a judge could only say, "You be hanged," whereas the bishop could say, "You be damned." "Ah" said Lord Salisbury, "but when a judge says 'You be hanged,' you are hanged."

DEMOCRATS AND REPUBLICANS

Will Rogers said it most eloquently: "I belong to no organized political party. I'm a Democrat.

■

The major difference between the two parties in America is when one does absolutely nothing, the other one always says they're doing it wrong.

■

A Republican is nothing more than a Democrat with richer friends.

■

There are only two political parties in America—the one you're aligned with, and the Know-nothing party.

■

There's no difference between a Republican and a Democrat. A politician by any other name would smell . . .

It doesn't matter if they're Republican or Democrat. If politicians like the working man so much, they would have become one.

■

Republicans and Democrats are all the same under the skin, and that's where they eventually get on most of us.

■

Democrats and Republicans are like alligators and crocodiles. Technically, there's a difference between them, but they're both dangerous.

■

As far as the average man on the street can tell, the main purpose of the two-party-system in America is to start arguments in bars.

■

A loyal Republican feels the Republicans can do no wrong; a true Democrat feels the Democrats can do no wrong. Somebody's screwing up the country.

■

True bipartisanship really works. It's the backbone of Democracy and the inspiration of all free nations. Unfortunately, it's usually used only when the House votes itself a pay raise.

■

Isn't it funny how the Democrats call the Republican crooks, and the Republicans call the Democrats crooks . . . and they're both right.

■

Both Democrats and Republicans should remember that no one party is large enough to hold all the crooks.

LIBERALS AND CONSERVATIVES

You can call a politician a liberal or you can call a politician a conservative. The only thing they really resent being called is a politician.

Politicians should have labels. If it's good enough for a can of peas on the shelf, it's good enough for them.

■

A liberal is someone who wants to spend money he doesn't have. A conservative is someone who wants to keep him from getting it.

■

The difference between a liberal and a conservative is this: If five people sit down to dinner and there are only four pork chops, the liberal says, "Great. That's one for everybody."

The conservative knows there's not enough for everybody to have one, so he just takes his two and starts eating.

■

Liberals want to save everybody else's money. Conservatives don't think anybody else should have money.

■

Liberals want a government of the people, by the people, and for the people. Conservatives just want to decide who those people should be.

■

Liberals want to feed the entire world. Conservatives do too, but they want to do it at a fund-raising dinner.

■

A liberal is a person who needs an interpreter when he speaks to William F. Buckley.

A conservative is a person who needs someone to hold his coat when he speaks to Ralph Nader.

■

Liberals want equality for all the people of the world. Conservatives do, too . . . but prorated by neighborhoods.

■

Liberals want to spread the wealth. Conservatives want to channel the wealth . . . into campaign funds.

Liberals live in a dream world. Conservatives don't like dreams because they can't be legislated.

■

Liberals believe in giving everyone a second chance. Conservatives believe in giving everyone a second mortgage.

■

A conservative is the guy who pulls up to the country club wearing gray slacks and a blazer with his family crest on the breast pocket and driving a spiffy new sports car. The liberal is the guy who parks his car for him.

■

Liberals want to preserve the great outdoors. Conservatives do, too, provided they can hire a gardener to care for it.

■

Liberals and conservatives basically want the same thing for the country. It's just that the liberals want the conservatives to pay for it.

■

If only the liberals and conservatives would learn to cooperate. For instance, freckles would be a nice tan if they'd get together.

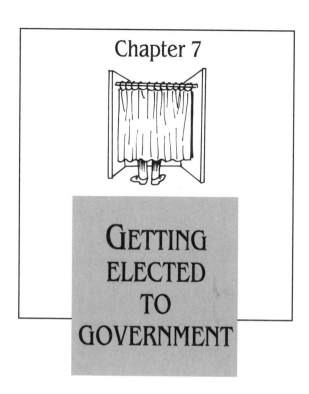

Chapter 7

GETTING ELECTED TO GOVERNMENT

CONVENTIONS

The political conventions last only a few days, and everybody usually knows how they're going to end. They're a lot like a Zsa Zsa Gabor marriage.

■

Most political conventions have all the suspense of playing Russian roulette with a bow and arrow.

■

Most political conventions need some excitement, something going on where nobody knows what's going to happen. They should have them start off with a Jerry Ford tee shot.

■

These political conventions are very dull, but the delegates try to make them exciting. They give all the speakers a standing yawn.

The political conventions are silly. They're like pajama parties for adults.

■

Most delegates go a little crazy at conventions. Something must happen to you when you pin on a nametag.

■

I don't know why people act so crazy when they go to conventions. They must put something in the airline food.
... it's certainly not nutrition.

■

A lot of drinking goes on at these conventions. They never run out of notepads or pencils—just swizzle sticks.

■

Some people spend the entire convention holding a drink in one hand. One delegate went to a convention in Phoenix in July and came home with frostbite.
... then he got another case of it when his wife met him at home.

■

I went to a hospitality suite once and thought it was an antifreeze convention.

■

In a hotel it's called a "Hospitality Suite." If it were on a street corner it would be called Saloon "a."

■

People sometimes get so light-headed at these conventions it causes the hotel problems. The elevators will only go up.

■

That's why everybody wears a name tag at these conventions. It's not so you'll know who the other people are tonight; it's so you'll remember who you are in the morning.

■

The delegates dress up silly at political conventions. I don't know what they're dressed for, but bobbing for apples would not look out of place at most of them.

One man wore a three-foot square of limburger cheese on his head. It didn't signify anything politically, but it did get him a good seat on the shuttle bus.

■

When you watch on television, you notice that all the delegates at political conventions are covered with campaign buttons. That's one reason why they rarely hold them at a nudist camp.

■

It's hard to believe that some of the people you see at the political conventions are the ones who are going to decide who's going to be our next President.

■

When our nation was conceived as a government "of the people, by the people, and for the people," I didn't realize all those people would be wearing funny hats at the convention.

CAMPAIGNING

The presidential campaign is starting up again. It's a shame. After the summer we've had, we don't need more hot air.

■

If you thought we had warm masses of air moving around the country this summer, wait till the campaign heats up.

■

I saw a very unusual sight the other day—a Democrat who wasn't running for President.

■

There's a simple rule of thumb that applies to politicians— anyone who isn't President wants to be.

■

The presidential candidates are starting to campaign early. They all want to declare before CBS projects a winner.

This is the time of year when politicians become like common people. They're looking for jobs, too.

■

In this campaign, some of the candidates are taking the bull by the horns. In politics, you have to do something with the bull.

■

All the presidential candidates love to get their pictures in the paper and to be on television. Some of them haven't taken off their make-up in four months.

■

Anytime a red light goes on they start giving a speech. One of them spoke for 25 minutes the other day in front of a house of ill repute.
Finally, one of the girls had enough sense to come out and unscrew the light bulb.

■

Every politician in Washington feels that everyone is incompetent except him. And he's generally right up until those last two words.

■

Politicians are funny. They'll do anything for a vote and then nothing after they get it.

■

Politicians really go after the voters. Politics is like kick boxing—strong supporters are so important.

■

Political campaigns are getting too organized lately. It's just not as much fun to have your baby kissed by a computer.

■

Only in America do people spend millions of dollars trying to get a job that pays $200,000 a year.

■

It costs over $15 million to put a person in the White House. That's a lot to spend considering all the people in Europe who go to bed each night without a president.

I guess it's worth it, but I get the feeling we should have waited for a sale.

■

It might be helpful to think of candidates as one of those balloons in the Macy's Thanksgiving Day Parade . . . bigger than life and full of hot air.

■

Candidates are always looking for a little publicity. One had a yellow sign in his car window that read, "Candidate on Board . . . In case of an accident, call a press conference."

■

The politician's wife just might have the hardest job on the campaign trail. Her role, as Jimmy Breslin described it is "to look adoringly at the politician when he talks and then to believe every lie he utters when he fails to get home at night."

CAMPAIGN PROMISES

Wouldn't it be a wonderful world if dreams came true—or even if campaign promises did?
Of course, that's pretty much the same difference, isn't it?
You tell a candidate, "Here's what you promised." He'll say, "You must have been dreaming."

■

I love campaign promises. They last about as long as a balloon at a porcupine's picnic.
I've had breath mints last longer than them.

■

Nobody keeps their campaign promises. That's why it's nice to lose the election—you have less to forget.

■

Campaign promises mean nothing. They're like a warranty on paper towels.

Campaign promises are like a ticket. You use them to get in, then you tear off a little piece and give it back.

■

The best way to get what you want is to vote for the guy who says he's not going to give it to you.

■

Campaign promises are a joke. They're the "dribble glasses" of politics.

■

A campaign promise is the political equivalent of "Yes dear, I will respect you in the morning."
Only the girl in that case is luckier. She doesn't have to face four years of those mornings.

■

Some people think Presidents should be elected for six years. Four years is not enough time to break all the campaign promises.

■

It happens every election. They tell us we can live on Easy Street, when all they want is to live on Pennsylvania Avenue.

■

The politicians get mad when their campaign promises come back to haunt them. They're trying to pass a law that all newspapers must be printed in disappearing ink.
. . . or at least in erasable pencil.

■

The election is the dividing point between things the candidate is going to do *for* you, and things he's going to do *to* you.

■

Election Day is like having the police raid your bookie's joint . . . from that moment on, all bets are off.

■

Most candidates back up their campaign promises by kissing a baby. This gives you a good idea of what kind of politician they will be; just watch to see which end they kiss.

Franklin K. Dane said, "I never vote for the best candidate; I vote for the one who will do the least harm."

■

The public likes when a candidate comes right out and says what he thinks, but only when he agrees with them.

DIRTY POLITICS

This is going to be a nasty presidential campaign. Both candidates are stooping to the truth.

■

All the candidates are preparing for the upcoming campaign. They're starting to arrange their mud into handy little sling-sized piles.

. . . Their teeth are in the shop getting sharpened up for the back-biting season.

. . . They're all out having their best suits mud-proofed.

■

You can spot the politicians who are gearing up for the upcoming election campaigns. Their fangs are beginning to grow longer.

They've been sucking in hot air for two years now and they're ready to let it all out.

■

Candidates really do a lot of name calling during the campaign. I turned on one of those presidential debates last week and thought I was watching "Divorce Court."

■

The presidential candidates finally talked issues during the debates. You know something? I prefer the name calling.

■

The presidential candidates finally had a few nice things to say about one another, but that doesn't mean much. You can't believe a politician.

You can't believe a political opponent when he says nice things about you. That's like getting a letter from the IRS that begins, "Dear Sir."

■

Most of us prefer politicians who are underhanded, double-dealing, back-stabbing, and two-faced. We've learned to trust them.

■

Hipponax the Satirist could have been describing today's dirty politics when he said, "Throw plenty of mud and some of it is bound to stick."

POLITICAL DEBATES

All the political rhetoric is starting on television. It's a nice time to set your roses in front of the TV set.

Remember the old days—when we used to have to get our fertilizer from real bulls?

■

I'm afraid the candidates are all going to be talked out after this campaign. This may be the first inaugural speech delivered in pantomime.

■

I'm glad politics isn't like baseball. I'd hate to see these presidential debates turn into a best-of-seven series.

■

Some bars won't allow you to talk politics. I think that ban should be extended to include presidential campaigns, too.

■

One of the candidates got a lot of applause during the presidential debate the other night. He vowed there would be no more debates.

■

I don't know why so many of us watch the presidential debates anyway. No one has to watch those debates . . . except, of course, Rich Little.

Rich Little wants to know who's going to win. He doesn't want to learn a new voice for no reason.

■

When debating, politicians should keep in mind the three secrets of success when speaking in public, "Be sincere, be brief, be seated."

■

During a debate one politician was asked, "Why is it that politicians always answer a question by asking one?"
"Do they?" was the politician's reply.

JOURNALISTS AND POLITICAL CANDIDATES

Newspeople investigate everything about the candidates nowadays. You run for office and they hold up X-rays of your childhood.

■

Everybody has a skeleton in their closet. The newspeople keep hoping it's in there fooling around with another skeleton.

■

If you do have a skeleton in your closet, *Playboy* and *Penthouse* will run nude photos of it in next month's issue.

■

It's not easy running for office nowadays. It's hard to wave to the crowd and cover your groin all at the same time.

■

Remember when LBJ used to stand for Lyndon Baines Johnson? Now it stands for "Low-Blow Journalism."

■

Newspeople really like to dig up dirt. They show up for press conferences with a notebook and a shovel.

■

Newspeople could dig up dirt on two eight-year old kids running for Cub Scout of the year.

The newspeople try to dig up scandals on all the presidential candidates. I guess they had such good luck with all the TV evangelists.

■

The news reporters are really starting to fight dirty. Someone should tell them they've got ring around the profession.

■

One politician threw a tantrum when he saw the lies a local paper was printing about him. The editor of the paper remarked, "I wonder what he would do if we told the truth about him?"

■

Emerson described democracy as a government of bullies tempered by editors.

THE POLLS

I don't know why the politicians rely so much on the polls. The polls do absolutely nothing. Wait a minute, I think I just answered my own question.

■

The polls not only tell us exactly what's going to happen, but when it doesn't they'll take another poll to tell us exactly what went wrong with the first poll.

■

Basically, polls are ineffective. That's why politicians like them so much.
. . . They have so much in common.

■

Do you know why George Washington was first in the hearts of his countrymen? Because they didn't have polls back then to tell him he wasn't.

■

The only things that are wrong more often than the political polls are some of the politicians they're measuring.

You show me a politician who says he doesn't believe in polls, and I'll show you a politician who's so far behind he's about to dump his campaign manager.

■

Some politicians say they don't believe in the polls. That's like a jockey telling you he doesn't believe in horses.

■

Everybody relies on the polls nowadays. I think the only reason they urge people to get out and vote is because it's the only way they have of telling if the polls were correct or not.

■

The polls tell the politicians what they should be doing. Remember the good old days when that used to be the job of the constituents?

■

The polls are there to let the politicians know what the little guy is thinking. It's like the general and colonel who were walking down the street. Every time they met a private, the colonel would salute and say, "The same to you."

Finally, the general asked, "Why do you always say that?"

The colonel answered, "I was once a private and I know what they are thinking."

■

A poll can be described as a place where you stand in line for a chance to decide who will spend your money.

VOTING

Voting is your voice in America, so speak up. But at least try to think before you speak.

■

Every politician wants your vote. The trick is to vote for those who don't want anything else that's yours.

■

We vote behind a curtain. With some of the candidates who run, no one would dare to vote for them in public.

Sometimes, don't you feel that we should vote in public and keep the people we elect behind a curtain?

■

It used to be in Chicago when they urged you to "vote, vote, vote," they meant it literally.

■

I, for one, have never wasted my vote. Although, with some of the people I helped elect, I came pretty damn close.

■

They say if you don't vote, then you have no right to complain. If that's true, how come only 50 percent of us vote while 100 percent of us gripe about our politicians?

■

Vote and send the best candidate to Washington—whether he wants to go or not.

■

Isn't it strange in some places you have to register to vote, but not to own a gun?

■

If your representatives are doing their job, vote for them. If your representatives aren't doing their job, vote against them. If you're not doing your job, don't vote.

———————■———————

"Vote early and vote often."

—Al Capone

"Take a look at what's happened in Eastern Europe. These people, some of them went out there in the streets and got beat up pretty bad just because they wanted to do something as simple as vote. And here you would have to take people out in the street and beat them up pretty bad to make them vote.

—Frank Zappa

THE ELECTIONS

The elections are over, and I don't know whether the Democrats or the Republicans won. It's always either the Democrats or the Republicans who win . . . never the people.

■

Elections are funny. We spend one day putting them into office and four years complaining about them.

■

A lot of candidates run out of money during the campaigns. That should be good training for running the country.

■

They really do a lot of name calling during the campaigns. I turned on one of the debates last week and I thought I was watching *Divorce Court*.

■

Of course, someone will eventually be elected. Then the other guys will immediately start running for the next election.

■

There are some people in politics now who feel it's their duty to tell the truth about their opponents . . . even if they have to make most of it up.

■

Television announces the projected winners so early we don't have an election day anymore. We have an election hour.

■

One candidate was so happy about winning he accidentally kept one of his campaign promises.

■

Some of our elections have been so one-sided that the next morning the losers' bumper stickers removed themselves.

■

Sometimes we just watch the election returns to see how long the anchor people can go without yawning.

There have been some one-sided elections in our history. Ones where the losing candidate didn't party at all, but just rested with a few intimate friends—the ones who voted for him.

■

We've had some elections that were so one-sided it was like Notre Dame playing against the Supremes.
. . . and Diana Ross was out with a sore elbow.

■

We've had elections that were so one-sided, the losing candidate didn't even have to ask for a recount. All he needed was a show of hands.

■

Some elections have been so lopsided, they had to wait for the absentee ballots to see if the loser carried his own household.

■

We had one presidential election that was so one-sided, NBC predicted very early that ABC and CBS wouldn't even cover it.

■

I like the philosophy of one old woman who said, "I never vote for any of them. It just encourages them."

■

Voting is your right and your privilege. Too often, it also turns out to be one of your regrets.

■

The Russians have been holding elections lately, too. It's not for any important offices . . . more like vice-president.

■

The Russians want to have political parties and conventions just like us. Why should the Americans be the only ones who get to wear funny hats every four years?

■

The Russians decided to hold elections because they watched our political conventions on television. For the first time they learned the real meaning of the word "Party."

Of course, all the Russian elections will be predetermined. Not like American elections; more like Chicago's.

■

The Russians want the people to get used to casting a ballot, but the winners will still be determined by the people in power. It's kind of like a cross between our political system and our wrestling on television.

■

In Russia, if you lose you don't make a concession speech. You give your farewell address.

■

The Russians want to be more democratic, something they haven't been for hundreds of years. Come to think of it, "Democratic" is something our White House hasn't had for a number of years, either.

■

The Russians are loosening up because they've got "Glasnost" and "Perestroika." They figure if they're going to have to learn to spell those words, they might as well mean something.

■

The Russians want to run their political machines as well as we run ours. In fact, they may send people over here to study how to make campaign buttons.

■

The Russian elections will be simple at first: "All those in favor, say aye; all those opposed report to the train with all your belongings."

■

In Russia, they have Siberia for the losers. In America, the closest thing we have to that is the Vice-President's office.

■

A farmer was detained for questioning about an election scandal. The U.S. attorney kept asking the farmer if he had sold his vote. The farmer kept replying that he voted for the fellow because he liked him.

Finally the attorney said, "I have good evidence that he gave you fifty dollars."

To which the farmer replied, "If someone gave you fifty dollars, wouldn't you like him?"

■

Gerald Barzan believes, "The only thing we learn from a new election is we learned nothing from the old."

———————■———————

Campaign resolutions are nothing more than overgrown New Year resolutions.

—W. C. Fields

The short memories of the American voters is what keeps our politicians in office.

—Will Rogers

Personally, I'm against political jokes. Too often they get elected to office.

—Henny Youngman

TV ELECTION RETURNS

Those TV election-return shows pick the winners too early. It's like going to a football game, and after the opening kick-off everybody gets up and leaves.

■

The networks are predicting the winners earlier and earlier. Pretty soon we'll just have one person go out and vote and have Dan Rather tell us who won.

■

After 1 percent of the vote is in, the networks tell us who won. It makes the other 99 percent of us feel a bit unnecessary.

■

How come the networks are so good at picking the presidential winner, and so bad at picking hit shows?

Voting for somebody who has already been announced as the loser is like betting on the eighth game of the World Series.

■

Those projected winners take all the excitement out of the voting. I think on election day they should open the bars and close the computers.

■

If you vote after they've already announced the winner, you feel dumb. It's like sending a wedding gift to Liz Taylor and Eddie Fisher.

■

If those computers are supposed to be so dependable, how come my charge bill gets fouled up every month?

■

I don't want a politician in office that was picked by a computer. I want one that I can fold, spindle, and mutilate.

■

I don't like to watch TV election returns. It's bad enough television tells me what toothpaste to buy. I don't want them also telling me who my next governor will be.

THE INAUGURATION GALA

The last inauguration gala cost more than $12 million. I had no idea party hats had gotten that expensive.

■

Can you imagine $12 million dollars for an inauguration ball? He's only going to be President, for crying out loud. It's not like it's his Bar Mitzvah.

■

Only a politician could have a party that big. They're the only people with enough hot air to blow up that many balloons.

Imagine spending $12 million for an inauguration gala. If they run out of cake and ice cream in the middle of it, they can always dip into the defense budget.

■

The inauguration party is generally spread out all over the city of Washington. It's a great kind of party. You can be halfway home and still be at the party.

■

It's nice to have a gala spread out over the entire city. No matter where you park, you're close to it.

■

There was a lot of security at Reagan's inauguration gala. It was to keep out terrorists and Democrats.

■

Ronald Reagan was the first to spend $12 million for his inauguration. I wonder what he would have spent if he ever won an Academy Award?

■

Inauguration galas serve a useful purpose. After all, this may be the last time anyone is glad that this particular person was elected President.

■

Eat, drink, and be merry. Tomorrow you have to start worrying about getting reelected.

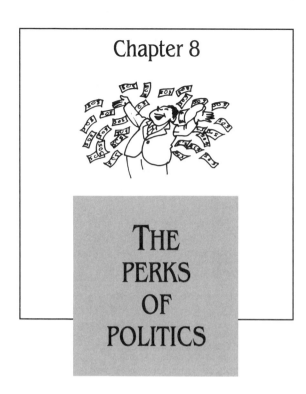

Chapter 8

THE PERKS OF POLITICS

CONGRESSIONAL CREDIT

Politicians get some pretty nice fringe benefits. That's because they're the people who write the fringes.

■

Congressmen have their own bank, which is pretty nice. You and I have to walk all the way to the corner.

■

Of course, this bank had very strict rules. After you've written 100 checks, you had to put some money in the bank.

■

The bank was never robbed. It didn't have to be. If you wanted all their money, all you had to do was get elected to Congress and write yourself a check.

In fact, when the members of Congress ordered their checkbooks, they got their choice of which color rubber they wanted.

■

Have you heard that Congress may investigate one of their own? They caught him passing good checks.

■

Congress had their own bank, which allowed them to pass bad checks. We're finding out that their checks are about as good as their campaign promises.

■

All these politicians are writing rubber checks. I guess it's no coincidence that the abbreviation for Congressman is CON.

■

They've been writing pure rubber checks. The only thing those checks are good for is erasing the numbers off other checks.

■

When a Congressman writes you a check, he says, "Here, roll this up in a ball and let the kids play with it."

■

The politicians don't understand what's wrong with writing bad checks. The government's been doing it for years.

■

It became Congress's new motto: "Foreign aid begins at home."

■

And members of Congress have their own restaurant. They could have good meals with bad checks.

■

You could order a bottle of their best wine and pay for it with your worst check.

■

Very few paid their bills in that Congressional restaurant. When they brought them their checks, they'd say, "Will that be cash, credit card, or just tear the damn thing up?"

No wonder the politicians don't think there's a recession going on. There isn't for anybody who can get free food and write all the bad checks he wants.

■

Members of Congress get free parking spaces at the airport. That's more than TWA gets.

■

They get free mailing privileges. They've got the softest job in the world, and they don't even have to lick stamps.

■

Talk about perks! A Congressman can pay his electric bill by sending a bad check in an envelope with no stamp.

■

Congressional credit is helping to solve the parking problem in Washington. Congressmen just buy a car on credit and leave it.

■

A woman once asked her Congressman why it was that he was never pressed for money and always seemed to have plenty of it?
"That is very simple; I never pay old debts."
"But surely you must have new ones?"
"I let them grow old."

POLITICS AND SHOW BUSINESS

Acting is the art of making people believe you really believe what you're saying. Isn't that what gets people elected, too?

■

Acting and politics are both make-believe. The only difference is, the actors know it.

■

Show business is similar to politics. In one you get applause, in the other you get junkets.
. . . The purpose of both is the same—to keep the people amused.

Politics and show business are alike in many ways. You don't really need ability, just to convince the people you have it.

■

Politics and show business are very much alike. The one big difference is when you do bad in show business it doesn't cost the taxpayers anything.

■

They are very similar except in show business you don't have to look who's behind you before taking your bow.

■

Show-business people do very well in politics. Lassie is even thinking of running for dog catcher.

■

A lot of old performers are going into politics nowadays. You do a bad show nowadays, the critics don't get after you; the party does.

■

There was a time when people retired from show business. Today, they're elected out.

■

I saw an old actor the other day. I said, "Are you running for office?" He said, "No, I'm just washed up."

■

There are a lot of old performers running for office today. When I watch the election returns nowadays, I get a craving for popcorn.

■

Washington, DC, is now known as Actors Equity East.

■

So many show-business people are making it in politics that Trigger may run for office. She figures government is about ready for a complete horse.

It's getting so that now old actors either collect unemployment or go into politics. They go on the government payroll one way or the other.

■

After show business, elections are easy. It's like going to an audition with only one other person trying out for the part.

■

I don't think we should have too many old performers in government, though. State dinners could turn into Friars' Roasts.

■

Show business is funny. You do a few bad shows and you could either be washed up or the next President of the United States.

■

The Hollywood unemployment office is the only place in the whole country where the guy in line behind you might say, "Can I get ahead of you? I have to rush out to a governor's conference."

■

Ronald Reagan was the first old actor to make it all the way. He looked around the White House and said, "Man, what a dressing room."

THE BOOKS POLITICIANS WILL WRITE

It's tough being President. Everybody in the administration leaves office and writes a book called *Mr. President Dearest*.

■

These sort of books used to be called "kiss and tell" books, but not anymore. It was too confusing. The public thought they were about television preachers.

■

They should pass a new law in Washington: Use a typewriter, go to jail.

Future presidents will be searching for the perfect staff—hardworking, loyal, prone to amnesia.

■

It's funny, a lot of the men who can't recall anything when questioned by Congress then go home and write a book about it.

■

Some of the politicians keep saying, "I don't recall" when being questioned. Then they have the nerve to call their book "memoirs."

■

They should do something about all those books. Make it a law that all typewriters in Washington, DC, have to have ribbons with disappearing ink.

■

You take the oath of office nowadays to serve your President and your country for the entire length of your term or for 80,000 words, whichever comes first.

■

I'd settle the "kiss-and-tell" book problem if I were elected President. I'd appoint only illiterates.

It makes sense. Our leaders have always been men who can read and write, and look at the mess the world is in today.

■

It's typing that's causing all the problems. I think once appointees raise their right hand to take the oath of office, they should never be allowed to bring it down again.

■

The reason some members of Congress are anxious to write a book is that they know they can't make a living in private business under the laws they passed while in Congress.

Chapter 9

THE COST OF GOVERNMENT

TAXES

Before the American Revolution, someone once said, "Taxation without representation is tyranny." With representation, its not that great either.

■

Taxes are necessary. So are shots, but no one enjoys them much either.

... and they hit you in about the same area.

■

There are two things that are unavoidable... death and taxes. Only death doesn't hurt more everytime Congress meets.

They're putting taxes on everything . . . smoking, drinking, driving. The only loophole is to remain quietly in your room.

■

They're taxing what they call the "luxury items." That means if you're in the United States and you're smiling, you owe money.

■

The rich get richer and the poor get poorer. That's an old saying. Now they're trying to make it a law.

■

They're trying to decide whether to tax the rich or the poor. Why don't they tax politicians?

■

I wish they would put the Pentagon in charge of taxes. Then when you deduct $700 for a new toilet seat, they'll believe it.

■

I have a great way of lowering income taxes tremendously. Each week your employer pays you what you're worth. Then, once a year you pay the government what they're worth.

■

Taxes . . . that's a government's way of saying, "Stick 'em up."

■

No, I always pay my taxes with a smile. They keep coming back and demanding cash.

■

Tax day . . . that's nature's way of telling you, "If you haven't spent it yet, you ain't going to."

■

They call it a "tax return" . . . that's a good word for it. You return all of their money you've been making.

■

They took a poll that says 6 out of 10 people cheat on their income taxes. That's probably higher because 8 out of 10 people cheat on polls.

I met one man who said he never cheats on his income-tax returns, but you can't believe a man who lies like that.

■

Even if we don't cheat, we all make honest mistakes on our income-tax returns. There are some people who really believe that the family dog is their daughter.

■

Every year they try to eliminate a few deductions. That doesn't mean the rich will pay more. It just means they'll have to work harder to pay less.

■

Whenever they cut deductions, people send their accountants scrambling to find other loopholes. H & R Block may have to hire another initial.

■

How can the government take away our deductions? That was the only fun of filing a tax return.
. . . it's like publishing *Playboy* without the dirty pictures.

■

The government will never outsmart the money people, though. While they're in Washington taking away the old deductions, the rich people are home thinking up new ones.

■

Remember one thing about money and taxes. You can't take it with you. The government is just trying to make it easier for you to pack for the trip.

■

They could end all our financial problems with a national lottery. The winner gets the Federal deficit.

■

I can always tell when tax time is near. My wallet breaks out in a cold sweat.

■

364 days a year it pays to be an American. On the 365th day, you pay to be an American.

April 15th is the day when you can look real close at a dollar bill and notice that George Washington's lips are puckered. He's kissing you bye-bye.

■

Tax day—that's nature's way of telling you: "If you haven't spent it yet, you ain't going to."

■

I hate to owe money at the end of the year. I hate to dig up the backyard just for that.

■

I used to feel bad about paying taxes until I looked at the federal deficit. The government is broker than we are.

■

I've got a foolproof tax shelter this year. My business manager ran away with my money.

■

Do you know why they call it a "return"? Because that's what they want you to do with all the money you've earned.

■

It's kind of barbaric to fill out a tax return every year. It's kind of like being kidnapped and then being forced to write your own ransom note.

■

Don't you love that instruction booklet? It's a 28-page stick-up note.

■

I think even the government is starting to be embarrassed by the amount of taxes they're charging us. They asked me to pay my taxes this year in small, unmarked bills.

■

Sears has a tax-consulting service right in the store. If you decide you can't pay your taxes, you can buy a sit-down lawn mower and try to make a break for Canada.

There are a lot of people now who claim they can save you a lot of money on your tax returns. Of course, you can only go to see them on visiting days.

■

One minute the government is thinking of raising capital gains taxes, and the next minute they're thinking about lowering them. I don't know whether to invest my money or bury it.

■

Politicians keep trying to decide whether to tax the rich or the poor. Why don't they tax politicians?

■

Evan Esar described taxpayers as "Some close their eyes, some stop their ears, some shut their mouths, but all pay through the nose."

■

Herman Wouk said, "Income tax returns are the most imaginative fiction being written today."

■

The IRS firmly believes that in this country every little child, no matter how humble his circumstance, can grow up and become a taxpayer.

■

Taxes . . . that's when your ship comes in, but the government unloads it.

■

Some politicians don't want the people to keep more money. They're afraid they'll just waste it on food, shelter, and clothing.

■

They say it may help the rich and hurt the poor. With the way taxes were before, we were all poor.

———————————■———————————

What is the difference between a taxidermist and a tax collector? The taxidermist takes only your skin.

—Mark Twain

Even when you make a tax form on the level, you don't know when it's through if you are a crook or a martyr.

—Will Rogers

Noah must have taken into the ark two taxes, one female and one male, and did they multiply bountifully.

—Will Rogers

I sent in my income tax last week but I didn't sign my name. I feel if I have to guess how much I'm going to make, then they can guess who it is.

—Dick Gregory

If the government really wants to simplify the tax forms, why don't they just print all the money with their return address on it.

—Bob Hope

If you owe the government five thousand dollars, you make out your return for ten thousand. The government owes you five, and you owe them five, so you're even.

—Gracie Allen

SIMPLIFIED TAXES

The politicians are always trying to make it easier for us to figure out how much we pay. I want them to make it easier for us to figure out how much we keep.

■

There's one very easy way for them to simplify taxes. Just print all the money in the form of a boomerang.

But that would be hard on Congress. They couldn't throw our money away as easily.

■

There should be a ban on tax simplifications. Figuring it out gets easier; paying it will always be hard.

Someday the politicians may make figuring out our taxes so easy that at H & R Block, the R may have to be laid off.

■

I know a great way to reduce taxes. We pay only what we can understand in the instruction booklet.

■

The old way made it easier to cheat on your taxes. The government couldn't understand the instruction booklet, either.

■

I think eventually government will come out with a real simplified tax form. It'll just say: "It's April 15th. You can keep any money that has your picture on it instead of George Washington's."

■

I'm afraid that someday they may come out with a very simplified tax form: "Send us whatever you've got. You can owe us the rest."

■

The IRS has come out with a real simplified tax booklet this year. You have to hire only three lawyers to read it.

Provided one of the lawyers can speak three foreign languages.

■

Scientists say people are living longer nowadays. They have to, just to figure out the simplified tax forms.

■

The new simplified tax forms just arrived in the mail. Who says blanks can't hurt you?

GOVERNMENT SPENDING

The government is spending more money than they have. Who do they think they are? Us?

We're spending too much as a nation. The next time I send my taxes in I'm going to mark the check "For Deposit Only."

■

Our government is just like us—they're spending more money than they have. The only difference is they don't have to pay taxes first.

■

The only thing in this world that moves faster than the speed of sound is other people's money in the hands of a politician.

■

Where is all this money going? Take a look at our major cities. They're certainly not using it to redecorate.

■

There's only one statue of a nonpolitician in our nation's Capitol building—Will Rogers. It's also the only statue of a man with his hands in his own pockets.

■

Anytime we prepare a bill to limit government spending, the politicians tear it up and throw it into their $4,035 wastebaskets.

■

Politicians like to spend. It's one of the few things they do well.
. . . and the only thing that both parties agree on.

■

I pay my taxes like everybody else. Well, maybe not like everybody else. I take a dose of laughing gas first.
. . . that explains why I always pay my taxes with a smile.

■

But I want my money to be used to run the government, not wasted. Wait a minute, it just dawned on me . . . those two are the same thing.

■

Our government lives by the words of George Bernard Shaw, when he said, "A government which robs Peter to pay Paul can always depend on the support of Paul."

CONGRESSIONAL PAY RAISES

Congress voted themselves a nice little pay raise. It must be nice to have a job where you don't *have* to believe in Santa Claus.

■

Congress, you know, votes on their own pay increases. That's a pretty nice way to ask the boss for a raise, isn't it?

■

And they don't send this vote to the people. It's too important an issue to trust to the masses.

■

Why should they let the people vote on their money? What do the people know about money? Half of them can't make ends meet.
   ... but we could if we voted on our own salaries like they do.

■

Wouldn't you like to have a job where you could vote your own pay raises? Now that's a fringe benefit with some teeth in it.

■

If I had a job like that I'd never spend any money. I'd be too busy voting.
   ... and counting.

■

It's nice to be able to vote your own pay raises. That's a better gimmick than marrying Johnny Carson.

■

It's a nice thing—being able to vote yourself a raise. That's like Phyllis Diller being able to give face lifts.

■

That's great, having a job where you can vote yourself a raise. That's like being born with your hand in the cookie jar.

■

If they can let Congress vote on their own raises, why not let us audit our own tax returns?

Imagine Congress being able to give themselves a nice pay increase. It's the opposite of foreign aid.

■

Congress has a strange way of holding the vote on pay increases. They say, "All in favor say 'Aye'; all opposed say 'Goodbye.'"

■

It's nice that Congress can vote themselves a pay increase. At last they found something that transcends party politics.

■

But Congress is always fair when they vote themselves a pay increase. They don't make it tax-free.

■

Congress voted themselves a hefty pay increase. They figure first they'll take care of their own personal finances, then they'll attack the budget deficit.

■

Congress has been so worried about the deficit that they voted themselves a pay raise. They said, "We want to get our fair share while there's still some to get."

■

I love when they vote themselves a pay raise. Congress says, "We can either reduce the deficit or be part of it."

■

Congress wants to make a lot of money now so that they'll be able to live up to the lifestyle they expect from their generous pensions.

■

Of course, we spent a fortune on some weapons that did no good; now we're spending it on politicians who do no good.

■

Politicians give themselves a raise because their theory is: You elected me, now you'll pay in more ways than one.

Congress voted themselves a nice pay increase. Their motto used to be "Government of the people, by the people, and for the people." That's been changed now to "Charity begins at home."

■

Sometimes they vote themselves raises of over 30 percent. That's a hefty increase for unskilled labor.

■

I'm against it. I think if politicians want a pay raise, the first thing they should do is get a job.

■

I don't know how we ever allowed Congress to vote their own pay raises. This should go down in history as the "I got mine; you get yours" bill.

■

I love Congress's attitude when they vote themselves a pay raise. They say, "Well, that takes care of our problems. Now what can we do for the rest of you folks?"

■

Voting themselves a pay raise is a new thing for politicians—trying to make extra money legally.

■

Ours is a government of the people, by the people, and for the people. They should have added "at the expense of the people."

■

I love the way Congress justifies their pay raise. They say, "We took a vote, and we think we're worth it."
. . . of course, we should look on the bright side. At least, we don't have to tip them.

■

You can't blame Congress too much. If I voted my own pay raises, I'd be Donald Trump right now.

■

It's nice being able to vote yourselves a raise. It sure beats earning one.

Congress defended voting themselves a pay raise by saying that it's a way to reach their constituents. Or was it to "touch" their constituents?

FOREIGN AID

Charity begins at home . . . unless Congress is in charge of it.

■

Politicians revise the age-old adage to read: "What's mine is mine; what's yours we'll give to some needy country."

■

Foreign aid is one of the great mysteries of our culture—why politicians would want to give money to people who don't even have a vote.

■

Foreign aid: That's Congress's way of saying, "Here, you take this. It's not my money anyway."

. . . Sometimes it seems as if they add: "There's plenty more where that came from."

■

Foreign aid: That's where Washington teaches our money to say "Bye-bye."

■

Our politicians spend so much on foreign aid, it's a wonder they still print our money in English.

I'm beginning to believe that "E Pluribus Unum" really means "First Come, First Served."

■

Our nation spends a lot on foreign aid. There must be better ways to get enemies than by buying them.

■

Some countries get very angry whenever we cut foreign aid. They say, "Go ahead. Keep making moves like that and pretty soon you won't have any enemies."

Congress sends our money all over the world. We not only have to pay our taxes, we also have to send along its carfare.

■

Over the years U.S. has come to stand for "Uncle Soft Touch."

■

We send our money everywhere. That's why they're known as Third-World nations. They get one-third of our money.

■

I don't mind paying my taxes, but I prefer it to be for one country at a time.

■

Many Americans are getting sick of all this foreign aid. They think whoever prints our money should mark it "For Domestic Use Only."

■

I sent my taxes in last year, and I attached a little note that read: "Try not to spend this all in one country."

■

Even the Russians keep asking us for money now. Have you noticed? They were cheaper when we didn't get along with them.

■

That's the first thing the Russians learned about democracy— how to ask for a handout.

■

We're finally learning what "Glasnost" and "Perestroika" mean—"Send money," and "Send more money."

■

We can't send foreign aid to Russia because we're faced with a deficit that would choke a horse. Russia says, "Send the money. We'll choke the horse for you."

■

The politicians say, "I think we should spread the money around a bit." You know how good politicians are at spreading stuff around.

THE BUDGET

Things look bad for the budget this year. The President sent his budget to Congress . . . collect.

■

Everybody knew things were going to be bad this year. The first item on the budget was $700,000 for red pencils for Congress.

■

This year, when each member of Congress got a copy of the budget, it had a tin cup attached.

■

Our budgets keep growing every year. Someday they're not going to tax us; they're just going to confiscate all our credit cards.

■

The budget was so enormous this year that the money was requested in small, unmarked bills.

■

There's only one sure way to get enough money in the government to cover the latest budget. Have everybody tell the truth on their tax returns.

■

Our budget keeps getting bigger every year. Last year we had more zeroes in our budget than we had in our government.

■

Our budget is getting too big. Last month, the President called me and asked for an advance on my taxes.

■

Have you seen our latest budget? I'm not used to seeing numbers that big on the front page. Normally, you generally read about them on the sports page.

■

Our budget is now into the trillions. A trillion is one with 12 zeroes behind it. That also sounds like the Los Angeles Rams football team.

A trillion dollars is hard to imagine. If you converted that to quarters, it would weigh about the same as Roseanne Arnold.

■

I'll try to make our budget easy for American shoppers to understand ... it would form a credit card the size of South America.

■

Some citizens don't really study the budget. They just want to know what their share is.
... and how they can avoid paying it.

■

The first thing Congress does after it gets the budget is cut everything. The President usually arrives on Capitol Hill in a limousine and goes back to the White House in a cab.

■

Politicians really enjoy arguing about the budget, though. It's funny, when you mention money, how their eyes light up.
... The only thing they enjoy more than talking about money is spending it.

■

Most citizens don't understand budgets and deficits. All we know is, everytime the politicians start to talk about them our pockets start to sweat.

■

I love the way the politicians fight over the budget. Some say we should do this, and some say we should do that. If they can't figure out what to do with my money, why don't they let me keep it awhile longer.
... at least when I've got it, I know what's best for it.

■

Our budget is so large, I just read about it and the credit cards in my wallet melted.

■

Our budget is so large, I don't know where all that money is going to come from. Although, I'm afraid I might find out on April 15th.

Every time England sees the size of our budget, they're kind of glad they lost the Revolutionary War.

I think our own government sees this budget and decides we can't afford ourselves.

■

Our government is operating at almost a $170 billion deficit each year. It's nice to know they live the way you and I do.

■

The budget's always a big fight in Washington. The Republicans battle the Democrats, and they use our money as weapons.

■

Everytime the politicians meet about the budget, they suggest something different. Who do they think they are—Phyllis Diller's plastic surgeons?

■

The politicians on Capitol Hill fight every year over the budget. If I had known my money was going to cause them this much trouble, I wouldn't have sent it to them.

■

It's hard for Congress to figure out how to spend money. For so many years, they've just been giving it away.

■

They try to save money by shutting down parks and monuments. Maybe if they just shut down Congress for a few days, the problem would solve itself.

■

You know what they say: Too many chefs can spoil the broth. I don't want them making lousy soup out of my money.

■

Fighting over the budget, the politicians try to tax the rich one day and the poor the next. I wish they'd make up their minds. I have to tell my accountant which one to make me.

The government has to cut spending. Of course, they are trying to cut back a little bit. Last time I looked, there were only three faces on Mount Rushmore.

■

The budget fighting is getting pretty serious. Capitol Hill is looking like something that would break out at a hockey match.

■

This budget fight is silly. I try to be a good American and pay my taxes each year with a smile . . . but now I'm starting to giggle.

THE DEFICIT

The United States owes more money now than anyone else in the world . . . with the possible exception of Willie Nelson.

■

We owe so much money we're going to change our national motto from "E Pluribus Unum" to "Put it on my tab."

■

Around the globe now we're known as "The land of the free and the home of the deadbeats."

■

It's getting so bad now that the first thing the President says when he answers the red telephone is, "The check is in the mail."

■

That's why our president stays home so much. He can't find a foreign country to visit that we don't owe money to.

■

That's good, though. When Japan finally takes over this country they can assume all our debts, too.

■

How can Uncle Sam run up a charge bill like that? He's not even married.

It's embarrassing. You look at a dollar bill closely. George Washington's cheeks are red from blushing.

■

Our national deficit has now reached over $300 billion. That's one helluva IOU.

■

Three hundred billion! That's almost enough to put together a professional basketball team.

■

It's dangerous to owe that much money to that many people. We may wake up one day and find the Statue of Liberty with both her legs broken.

■

I don't know what the government has bought for $300 billion, but next time I wish they'd wait till it was on sale.

■

Every man, woman, and child in the United States owes $35,000. A kid is born today, he gets a rattle and a bill for $35,000.

You don't even have to spank a newborn nowadays to make him cry. Just show him his share of the national debt.

■

It must be tough on a newborn to come into the world and owe $35,000. Where was he before he was living for free?

■

You and I owe $35,000 . . . and it's not even the end of the month yet.

■

When we pledge allegiance to the flag now we should hold our hand over our wallets.

■

I owe the government $35,000. And I thought my bookie was bad.

It's terrible. You have to hit the lottery nowadays just to break even.

■

I don't understand how I can owe the government $35,000. What have they been doing with all the money I've been giving them all these years?

I've paid Washington thousands of dollars over the years, and I'm still $35,000 short. I could have done better going to a loan shark.

... as if there's a difference.

■

Sometimes our deficit gets so bad that the President's State of the Union address is typed in red ink.

■

Every year our deficit seems to get bigger and bigger. Pretty soon we're going to have to start renting out the empty rooms in the White House.

■

Our deficit is growing so fast that pretty soon we may qualify for foreign aid.

■

The only way now for our country to get out of debt is to declare war on ourselves and lose.

■

Our national deficit is growing so fast that pretty soon we may call England and volunteer to become "the Colonies" again.

■

We do have to keep a rein on that deficit. We fought hard for our independence. We'd hate to have the country repossessed.

■

With our deficit, the government shows definite signs of running out of money. Who do they think they are—us?

■

Politicians love the deficit because it's all interest. They don't even have to spend it; it spends itself.

We have a pretty big deficit. Remember how many pages were in your last telephone directory? Multiply that by 26 billion.

■

Our nation's interest payments have tripled since 1979. That's what happens when you buy a country on time.

■

America is a great country to live in, but I always thought it was paid for.

■

Our deficit is getting so bad, we can't even afford the red ink it takes to write it.

■

We're in such bad shape financially that our next state dinner is being paid for with food stamps.

■

It's hard to understand a deficit this large. It's as if you lost your charge card and Zsa Zsa Gabor found it.

■

The interest payments on our deficit alone are now over $111 billion. That's also the number of opinions we have on how to handle it.

■

No two politicians agree on what to do about the deficit. It's amazing how they can find that many different fences to straddle.

■

The deficit is getting out of hand. The government may stop printing money and start printing credit cards.

■

It seems that every citizen has an opinion on what to do about the deficit. Maybe that's how we can raise the money we need—charge $1 to everyone who wants to give advice.

We do owe a lot of money. You know this great land of ours from sea to shining sea? Well, it's all being used as collateral.

■

Of course, this deficit is a nice feeling for the little guy. Anybody who can afford to pay his bills each week is richer than the country.

■

We're in financial trouble because of this deficit. Our government is nervous because they're spending more than they take in. So what? All of us do, only the government doesn't have to pay taxes on it.

■

If we need more money, why don't we just print more money. That's what my Uncle in Iowa does, and so far it's worked for him.

■

Herbert Hoover had this to say about our deficit: "Blessed are the young, for they shall inherit the national debt."

■

One politician says he doesn't want foreign money buying up American businesses. With the deficit we have, that's the only kind of money we have.

■

We have a lot of foreign money over here now. My bank just put a sign in their window that says, "English Spoken Here."

THE COST OF DEFENSE

Even though our country's free, it costs a lot to keep it that way.

■

Our defense costs quite a bit. Peace and freedom are high-ticket items.

Defense costs a lot in our country. I mean defense of our country, not the legal defense of our elected officials.

■

We have to stay ready. In case of an emergency you don't have time to rent a tank from the "U-Fight-It" company.

■

One stealth bomber costs $500 million . . . and that's not including taxes and dealer prep.
. . . and, of course, power steering and air conditioning are extra.

■

The stealth bomber is shaped a little bit like a boomerang, which is reassuring. At 500 million bucks, you want to make sure it comes back to you.

■

The stealth bomber is just a flying wing with no tail. If you want one with a tail, it costs $600 million.

■

The stealth bomber is invisible to radar. I don't know . . . at $500 million apiece, I think I'd want everybody to know I was coming.

■

The plane is invisible, but the price tag hanging from the wing can be seen for miles.

■

If the stealth bomber is invisible, why don't we save some money—not buy any and just tell our enemies they're up there?

■

That's typical of the government, though . . . to spend half a billion dollars on something that nobody can see.
I wish they'd make cars that were invisible. At least then the freeways wouldn't *look* as crowded.
It would be nice to have invisible cars, wouldn't it? You could drive by, and people would just wonder what's holding up your bumper stickers.

Cutbacks in defense just don't work. GI's say chipped beef just doesn't taste the same without the shingle.

■

Our military proved they were ready in the Persian Gulf War. Any outfit that can fight that well with sand in their shorts . . .

■

Most of our defense budget goes toward high tech equipment. Anyone who's been in the service knows it doesn't go toward food.

. . . or cook books.

The chef in one army unit was quite famous for his 30-millimeter biscuits.

■

The navy spends a lot on jet fuel. It's the secret ingredient in their beans.

■

The cooks don't have to be very good in the navy. It's very hard to tell food poisoning from seasickness.

Of course, there is one way—if you have to pick a number to get to the railing after meals, it's the food.

■

If you can, you should pick up a recipe for the navy's biscuits. It might come in handy if you ever have to repave your driveway.

■

You know where the military chefs learn to make their gravy, don't you? At camouflage school.

■

Even though the food is sometimes bad in the military, the GI's wolf it down like crazy. They figure if we don't eat it all tonight, we'll just get it again tomorrow.

■

One general told me the enlisted personnel eat the same food as the officers in the military. It's just that the enlisted men get it two or three days later.

They cut costs by having a lot of stew in the service. Stew is a military term meaning, "Don't feed it to the officers until one of the enlisted men tries it first."

■

I once got the recipe for a military chef's stew. It began: Take the ingredients from last week . . .

■

We need a strong army. Only a strong military on KP duty will ever get those pots clean.

LOTTERIES

Lotteries are something. With just one drawing they can take an ordinary person and make him rich enough to marry Zsa Zsa Gabor.

. . . of course, you have to win two or three more times to become rich enough to divorce Zsa Zsa Gabor.

■

Whoever wins the lottery gets two prizes—a lot of money and a pen pal at the Internal Revenue Service.

■

You know what state lotteries are. They're drawings that give away a lot of money to people who don't even play baseball or basketball.

■

When you win the lottery, you not only get a lot of money, but you get to meet a lot of relatives you never had before.

■

Of course, there is a bad side when an ordinary person wins the lottery. The next year, H & R Block charges you a little more for your tax return.

■

I knew they'd get around to inventing it sooner or later—instant money.

It must be nice to make that much money instantly, without having to put on a ski mask or anything.

■

It's pretty great to have the government give you millions of dollars just because they pick your name out of a hat. Of course, for years that's also how they drafted you.

■

It must be nice to get a big check in the mail each month without doing anything. It's kind of like alimony without the marriage.

■

It must be nice to get money from someone for doing nothing. It must make you feel like the IRS.

■

Of course, we have a lot of millionaires today. At every basketball game there are five on a side.

■

These lotteries are something. You give money to the state and you've got an outside chance of getting something back. It's exactly the same in states where they don't have lotteries.

■

Of course, right after you win the lottery you get a letter from the government saying, "Congratulations, Partner."

■

There's only one sure winner in all these lotteries—the IRS.
Your chances of winning are about 1 in 14 million. The IRS's chances of winning are 1 in 1.

■

Remember the old days when the states used to arrest people who ran lotteries?

■

Lotteries are the second biggest form of government gambling. The first is elections.

I like the lotteries. I think it's nice for a change to see governments giving money to people in *this* country.

■

You get this money for doing nothing. It's almost like being in politics.

■

Can you imagine ordinary people winning all this money in a state lottery? I break out in a rash when I win a free Egg McMuffin at McDonald's.

■

Winning a state lottery! Boy, that's a great way to make several million dollars, isn't it? Come to think of it, there are no *bad* ways to make several million dollars.

■

I wonder if winning that kind of money changes your life. If it doesn't, you're doing something wrong.

■

At one time, the California lottery was up to $120 million. The time will come when somebody will win the lottery and not get any money; they'll just own California.
. . . that sounds like a good deal at first, but how'd you like to be stuck with that gardening bill?
. . . you'd be rich, but you'd have to spend the rest of your life mowing the grass.

■

Personally, I don't think it's right for one person to win that much money in a lottery. I'd rather get it back as a refund on my tax return.

■

It's natural that governments would go into the lottery business, though, because buying a lottery ticket is almost like throwing your money away. And governments are expert at that.

■

Many governments have decided to make money off people who love to gamble. That's a real switch—the government watching other people throw money away.

They say the odds of winning the lottery are about the same as getting hit by lightning, except that after getting hit by lightning, you can't go to work the next day and tell your boss to "sit on it."

■

If you win the lottery, everybody would have advice telling you what to do with your money. And you'd be so rich, you could afford to tell them what to do with their advice.

■

Winning that kind of money would allow you to say the kinds of things you've probably been wanting to say all your life—like, "Have you got change for a $20,000 bill?"

■

One state even tried to legalize betting on National Football League games. It's pretty nice to have the entire state as your bookie.

What happens if you run up a big gambling debt? Does the state attorney general come around and break your legs?

■

Some say sports gambling is a sordid business and shouldn't be mixed in with government. Let's keep all of our sordid business separated.

Besides, governments can control the outcome of the games too much. If one side is winning, in the second half, their star quarterback could suddenly be appointed Ambassador to Istanbul.

■

Betting could become so commonplace that football could be similar to horse racing. Then I feel sorry for the first player who breaks his leg on the field.

■

Government doesn't need sports gambling. They've got enough illegal activities going for them already.

■

Sports gambling and government should be kept separate. Otherwise, "Bagman" could become an elective office.

Of course, I don't like betting with the government, anyway. Once they pay off their bet, they take half of it back in taxes.

■

I don't like dealing with a bookie who has the power to condemn your house.

■

I think dealing with the government is enough of a gamble already without adding football scores.

■

Football is a game, and it should be left that way. In fact, maybe we should turn government into a game, too.

■

Football and politics are totally different. In football, if you do something wrong, they penalize you immediately. In politics, it takes four or five years to investigate them.

. . . by that time, nobody remembers they committed it.

Chapter 10

THE PROBLEMS OF GOVERNMENT

THE ECONOMY

Politicians can always talk about the economy. We may be running out of money, but we've still got plenty of words.

... It's nice to know that even with today's economy, talk is still cheap.

■

Everybody in America is trying to cut expenses ... except the government.

■

Interest rates have come way down. You can now borrow money without proving that you're richer than the bank.

Banks are cutting back on everything lately. I just got my Christmas calendar. It only has four months in it.

■

Banks are paying nothing now. I've had a savings account at my bank for over 20 years. They called last week and want their free toaster back.

■

The banks are giving absolutely nothing away for free. My local branch now has coin-operated ball-point pens.

■

Banks are trying to stimulate the economy by cutting interest rates. Our economy doesn't need stimulation; it needs mouth-to-mouth resuscitation.

■

The drop in interest rates is supposed to stimulate credit. They're trying to get people to buy things with money they haven't got. The trouble is the people are afraid they're going to have to pay for it with money they're not going to get.

■

The cost of borrowing money was so high for awhile that people couldn't get a loan because of medical reasons. Everytime they heard the interest rates they got a nosebleed.

WHEN THE DOLLAR'S STRONG

The dollar is very strong overseas . . . which is good for me. That's how much I usually travel with.

■

You can get some good bargains overseas now. Some tourists are arriving with one suitcase and going home with one suitcase, a tote bag, and two pack mules.

■

People are buying so much when they go overseas now that the airplanes fly home pulling a U-Haul trailer behind them.

The dollar is so strong overseas now that you can fly to London to meet girls. It's cheaper than a singles bar.

■

The dollar is so strong overseas now that there are a lot of tourists taking advantage. Some people are flying to Europe now just to meet Americans.

WHEN THE DOLLAR'S WEAK

The dollar has been devalued again. It's a terrible feeling to sit in your room and watch the wallet on your dresser lose weight.

■

You remember the dollar . . . the latest version of the Edsel.

■

The dollar is worth so little now that banks don't even lock up at night.

■

The south is happy. Every day the value of the dollar gets closer and closer to Confederate money.

■

Our dollar is shrinking so fast that the new bills being printed will show George Washington when he was a boy.

■

It's hardly worth the ink to print the dollar anymore. The next ones issued are going to be the paint-by-number variety.

■

The dollar keeps going down, and meat prices keep going up. It may be worth it to sell your wallet and buy a food locker.

■

The dollar is shrinking so fast that those Indians who bought New York for beads worth $24 are beginning to show a profit.

As youngsters we thought money was the most important thing in life. As adults, we're sure of it.

■

Our economy has gotten so bad. There once was a time when a fool and his money were soon parted, but now it happens to everyone.

RECESSION

Slappy White may have said it best: Times are so bad right now that even people who don't intend to pay aren't buying.

■

Times are tough during a recession. Even the rich people have to tighten the cinches on their polo ponies.

■

Times are really getting bad. *Woman's Day* is now publishing recipes for dogfood.

■

It's hard to explain a recession to wealthy people. Let's put it this way: Do they realize there are people who have to count before they buy something?

■

The wealthy are affected only by a *serious* recession. Serious recession—that's when your polo pony starts looking delicious.
     ... that's when you'd like to trade in your fur coat for the meat that used to be inside it.
     ... that's when the upper middle class is anybody with a job.

■

Times are so bad now that some of us can even afford to tell the truth on our tax returns.

■

Times are tough. People used to try to make their money last till the end of the month; now they're trying to do the same thing with their beef stew.

People don't spend much during a recession. When clerks ring up an item in a department store, they say, "Will that be cash, credit, or never mind?"

■

I was shopping once when the cash register rang and they closed the store for a celebration.

■

During a recession people are just looking; they're not buying. One department store reported its highest earnings for the past quarter were from the coin-operated restrooms.

■

One department-store chain is doing so badly they've qualified to use their own handicapped parking spaces.

■

Nobody's buying anything. Even shoplifters are leaving the stores empty-handed.

■

One department store had a sign that advertised a special recession sale. It advertised "25% off everything." One shopper turned to another and said, "Only 75% more to go."

■

During a recession there's just not that much money around. If the stores hear loose change rattling in your pocket, you're entitled to free cocktails and finger sandwiches in the VIP lounge.

Stores have sales clerks who are trained to follow anyone around the store who has a warm credit card on her person.

■

Stores just don't do much business during a recession. The stores are open late, but people's wallets aren't.

■

I walked into a department store during the recession. A salesman shook my hand, and his pet leech attached itself to my wallet.

You especially feel the recession around Christmas time. I saw one department-store Santa Claus telling another department-store Santa Claus what he wanted for Christmas.

■

Everybody tries to cut corners. I knew one guy who even bought a Volkswagen that was made in Japan.

■

The recession is getting pretty bad. If money were food, our economy would be chipped beef on toast.

■

The recession has even reached Hollywood. The only actors who are working steady are the ones who've been elected to something.

■

The studios are cutting back on everything. Charlton Heston may make a movie next year called "The Four Commandments."

■

A lot of actors are out of work. You walk along the streets of Hollywood and panhandlers will come up to you and say, "Can I have a dollar for a cup of coffee and ten cents for my agent?"

■

The studios are cutting back on budgets. If a certain western were made this year, it would be called "Butch Cassidy *or* the Sundance Kid."

■

I watched a western the other day where a posse chased the baddies out of town, and they all rode the same horse.

■

Recession . . . that's when people get the feeling they don't belong . . . the house doesn't belong to them, the car doesn't belong to them . . .

■

Recessions hurt everyone. Like the time during the Depression when Babe Ruth was asked to submit to a salary cut. He insisted on his usual fee. "But Babe," protested the Yankee official, "these are hard times. You're asking for more money than Hoover got last year for being President of the United States." "But," persisted Babe, "I had a better year than Hoover."

■

One problem that causes recession is that people stop living within their income and start living within their credit.

INFLATION

Inflation is when prices go from reasonable, to expensive, to "How much have you got with you?"

■

Inflation is like a balding man going to a hair stylist—he keeps paying more and more for less and less.

■

Inflation has driven the value of our money down so much that now even muggers won't accept cash.

■

They used to say that money can't buy happiness. Today it can't even buy groceries.

■

Vending machines used to take nickels, dimes, and quarters. Now they take down payments.

And the candy bars keep getting smaller. I opened one the other day and all I got was a chocolate-covered IOU.

■

You know inflation is bad when your pay envelope is trimmed in black.

■

Inflation is so bad now, your pay envelope comes with nothing in it but a deduction statement and a sympathy card.

■

I asked my wife the other day to hand me the comics. She gave me the financial page.

Food prices are pure robbery. One supermarket even has stockings pulled over its heads of lettuce.

■

Inflation is so bad now that some people go to the supermarket just to get an estimate on dinner.

■

It's a terrible feeling nowadays when you see the prices that the cash register rings up at the supermarket. That's why they don't keep razor blades near the checkout counters anymore.

■

Food prices are so high nowadays it's easy to spot the upper-middle class. They're the ones who remember how to chew.

■

Food prices are supposed to rise another 10 percent soon. Remember the food you couldn't afford last month? Well, now you can't afford only 90 percent of it.

■

Food prices are out of sight. Every food market check-out counter now has an anesthesiologist.

■

Food prices are so ridiculous, when you check out now the clerk asks, "Will that be cash, credit, or just try to make a run for it?"

■

Prices just keep going up and up. Pretty soon, it's going to be: Anything you can afford is a luxury.

■

Inflation cuts down on the economy. With most people if you can afford it, you probably wouldn't want it anyway.

■

With inflation, a lot of people are asking their bosses for a raise. Like the woman who went to her boss and demanded a raise. She said, "I'll have to have a raise, sir. There are three companies after me."
"What three?" asked the boss.
"The light, telephone, and water."

The effects of inflation are obvious when you realize it costs more now to amuse a child than it used to cost to educate his father.

■

Maybe the President won't be able to cure poverty, but with inflation, he sure is doing a good job of curing wealth.

UNEMPLOYMENT

Some people think that unemployment means not working. There are a lot of people in this country who are not working . . . but getting paid for it.

■

The one good thing about unemployment is that you do have fewer payroll deductions.

■

Politicians know a lot about unemployment. In fact, they'd like to change it into an elective office.
. . . as if it isn't already.

■

Unemployment wouldn't be so bad if it paid better.

■

A lot of people I know aren't working. The guy who is supposed to be fixing my car, the plumber who said he'd be here by noon, and the scientist who is supposed to discover a cure for baldness.

■

Some people are unemployed because they choose to be. Like my brother-in-law won't take any job unless his employer promises to pick up and deliver.

■

I like the politician who said, "I'm going to try to get jobs for all of our unemployed." Who else would he want to get jobs for?

■

My brother-in-law says unemployment wouldn't be so bad if only there were more opportunity for advancement . . . He wants to be the supervisor of people out of work . . . Maybe even regional manager.

Politicians never recognize the seriousness of unemployment. All their friends are working.

■

One politician promised the unemployed that he would get them all work. They said, "We want you to help us, not punish us."

■

Unemployment is a national curse. Of course, for some of us, employment isn't that hot, either.

■

The unemployment problem could be solved if only we had more unemployed politicians.

■

Unemployment isn't on the rise. It's just that there is a downward trend of an upward tendency.

CRIME AND VIOLENCE IN AMERICA

Crime in the streets is so bad, one man said to his wife, "I'm going out to pick up the paper. Cover me."

■

Violence is a part of America. The Los Angeles freeways now have places where you can pull over to reload.

■

They have speed bumps in California now. They're not to slow down the car; they're to throw off your aim.

■

Crime has gotten so bad. Nobody asks you for the time, they just take your watch.

The courts release people easily today. One reason we have so much crime in the streets is because that's where most of the prisoners are.

■

Criminals should be behind bars. It gives them time to write their best-selling books.

■

Most politicians say they'll be tough on criminals . . . except perhaps, those in their own administration.

■

When men are pure, laws are useless; when men are corrupt, laws are broken.

—Benjamin Disraeli

VIOLENCE IN FILMS

Movies today are too graphic. You wonder how they ever made films before blood was invented.

■

There's too much violence and crime in movies today. I saw a film last week that was rated "X" by the Mafia.

■

You used to be able to tell a movie hero because at the end he got the girl. Today at the end of a movie, he still has all his body parts.

■

Movies today are getting too violent. The Internal Revenue Service today allows gangsters to deduct theater tickets as research.

■

Film violence sells a lot of popcorn, though. Today's movies are so sickening, you're going to need the empty bag anyway.

■

There's violence in all the movies made now. If Lassie came home today, she'd have a dead chicken in her mouth.

Studios don't hire extras anymore; they hire blood donors.

■

Kids today want to become movie stars so they can see their blood type up in lights.

■

Producers used to hire people based on their acting ability. Nowadays, they just want good bleeders.

■

All today's movies do is kill people. The names of the actors at the end of the movie is now known as the "Cast of Cadavers."

■

If an actor is alive at the end of a picture today, it means he forgot his lines.

■

Everybody gets beat up in films nowadays. The costuming award this year may go to Ace bandages.

■

In one movie I saw they actually show someone reaching into a guy's chest and pulling his heart out. It's dangerous showing things like that. The IRS might see it.

■

The old movies were pleasant, but today's movies are violent. If it were made today, *A Face in the Crowd* wouldn't have a body attached to it.

. . . *Miracle on 34th Street* would be about a guy who walked from 33rd to 35th without getting mugged.

. . . *Gone With the Wind* would be about a man who was cremated in Chicago.

. . . *National Velvet* would be a documentary about casket linings.

. . . *A Tree Grows in Brooklyn* would fall on somebody.

. . . *Going My Way* would be the story of a door-to-door undertaker.

Movie violence in the old days was showing a Lassie film without having one fireplug in it.
... It was showing Tarzan running naked through the jungle ... before Calamine lotion was discovered.

■

People are flocking to see all the violent movies. I guess the evening news isn't enough for them.

■

Violent movies are really popular. "Best Supporting Actor" last year went to a chainsaw.

■

Violent movies are making money hand over fist ... which is the same way they usually strangle the heroine in scene three.

■

Whatever happened to the good old days when if people wanted violence they just went shopping during the January white sales?

VIOLENCE ON TELEVISION

I think they should ban all violence from television. I didn't want to see the political conventions this year anyway.

■

Take all the guns away from television and what have you got? A lot of people bleeding for no apparent reason.

■

TV crime and violence are affecting our youngsters. Kids used to ask for a nickel for candy; nowadays they ask for a nickel for ammunition.

■

Because of TV, all over America kids are uttering their first words—"Bang-bang."

■

Kids are affected by all that violence they see on TV. You ask a youngster what he wants to be when he grows up, he'll say, "A survivor."

Violence in Football

Football gets more and more violent every week. It looks like a demolition derby where they all forgot to bring their cars.

■

Professional football is a violent sport. It's like trying to cross the freeway at midnight in a black suit.

■

The players now wear their numbers on their sleeves, their trousers, their helmet. That's so after they get pulled apart, they'll know which pieces go where.

■

Everybody is getting hurt in football lately. I even saw one of the cheerleaders with sprained pom-poms.

■

One player had an upset stomach after the game. It came from eating too many noses.

■

I watched one professional football game. There were 22 men on the field and only 3 good knees.

■

One player had a 100-yard game last week. And that was just from being carried on and off the field.

■

They fix those injured players up and send them right back into the game. The trainer for one team is Mr. Goodwrench.

■

One guy was penalized 15 yards for "illegal use of his crutch."

■

One professional lineman was listed as weighing 280 pounds. When they took off all the tape and bandages, he weighed 135 pounds.

■

I don't know how they get all that tape off. I need three guys to hold me down when I take off a Band-Aid.

THE DRUG PROBLEM

Some people want to legalize drugs in America. They also want to make "Fly Me to the Moon" our national anthem.

■

I'm not for legalizing drugs. If we do that, soon the entire country will smell like a rock concert.
Besides, it could ruin baseball games. Pop flies would never come down.
. . . although some players might go up and meet them halfway.

■

No, sir, I don't want to legalize drugs in this country. Our airways are already crowded enough.

■

We have a serious drug problem. Some kids take drugs because they say it helps them find themselves. I never knew I was lost.

■

Yeah, some people say they're taking drugs because it helps them find themselves. The problem is they're so spaced out, when they find themselves, they're not even sure it's them.

■

Some college kids take drugs because they say it's an aphrodisiac. It puts them in touch with themselves and anyone else that happens to be walking by at the time.
. . . Any college kid who needs an aphrodisiac today isn't reading the right magazines.

■

Some college kids say they simply use drugs as an aphrodisiac. Aren't co-ed dorms aphrodisiac enough?

■

A recent report said that 40 percent of the people on our highways are on drugs. That may explain why 20 percent of them don't have cars.

It's frightening, isn't it? Four out of ten drivers that you pass have as their co-pilot Puff the Magic Dragon.

■

Forty percent of today's drivers can travel from Los Angeles to San Francisco without once leaving the Age of Aquarius.

■

Today's cars are equipped for these drivers. They have first gear, second gear, and mellow.

■

Some of today's drivers are so spaced out that when they put their arm out the window to signal, you're not even sure the window's open.

■

It must be true. I passed a guy last week trying to change a tire using a roach clip.

■

Everybody's on drugs. Even some of our cough medicines are so strong they can be prescribed only by your local drummer.
. . . I've taken some cough syrups that have knocked me flat on the ceiling.

■

Even cough medicines have drugs in them. One comes in three convenient forms . . . syrup, tablets, and roll your own.

■

Read the label on some of the nonprescription stuff sometime. It says, "Not to be taken by children, people with high blood pressure, or anyone who is afraid of floating."

■

Some of those commercial products are so powerful, the last thing you remember doing is taking the cotton out of the bottle.

■

They come with a recommended dosage and a little piece of paper that contains instructions for landing.

And doctors can prescribe some powerful stuff, too. They give you drugs that make you feel so good you don't even mind paying their bill.

■

Some of them don't even try to hide it. I had a prescription filled once and the instructions on the label read: "Score once before meals."

■

You really float on some of today's sleeping pills. You can get a good night's sleep, wake up the next morning, and the bed's not even mussed.

■

There are a lot of drugs in sports. You can't tell the players now without a prescription.

■

Athletes are turning to drugs for help. Steroids have become the new athletic supporter.

■

Steroids are body-building drugs. If a normal person takes drugs, he turns into a weight lifter. If a Russian woman track star takes steroids, she turns into a truck.

■

Steroids can make you impotent. So even if you do win a gold medal, how are you going to celebrate?

■

Steroids can make you run fast, but they can also make you impotent. I'd rather walk and have more fun when I get there.

■

They say there are a lot of drugs in sports, but I don't know . . . just because the pole vaulters don't use poles anymore.

■

I think there are drugs in sports. Either that or they're importing their urine from Columbia.

Athletes are using marijuana, crack, cocaine. There used to be a time when they got in trouble just for using too much pine tar.

■

Some of our athletes have so many drugs in them they have to wear tamperproof warm-up suits.

■

One athlete can do the 100-yard dash in 10 seconds flat. But he can make it to the pharmacy in 9.3.

■

One athlete had so many pills in him when he ran the hurdles he rattled.

■

One athlete was so loaded with drugs, he belched at the starting line and the guy next to him hallucinated.

■

The hardest part of the pole vault now is trying to get the athletes to come down again.

■

Remember the good old days in baseball when a foreign substance used to mean spit?

■

I went to the game the other day and asked the vendor if he had any Coke. Six of the players came out of the dugout with their hands up.

■

In the old days they used to have to watch the players to make sure they didn't spit on the ball. Now they have to make sure they don't smoke it.

■

Many of the baseball players prefer real grass to the artificial. They say it doesn't leave an aftertaste.

■

A lot of the players are catching pop flies now before they come down.

In football they've added another referee. Besides the head linesman and the field judge, they also have the undercover agent.

■

They're uncovering some drug usage in football. They became suspicious when a lot of the players came out of the huddle happier than when they went in.

■

Not too many golfers use drugs. It's hard enough finding your way out of the woods sober.

■

You really can't take drugs and play golf at the same time. It's hard enough to hit the ball when it's just standing still.
... Besides, it's difficult to putt when you're feet don't touch the ground.

■

Then again, it might come in handy. The rules say you can't remove a natural obstacle, but it doesn't say you can't smoke it.

■

The only chemical that would drastically affect golf would be truth serum.

■

It would be too easy to spot golfers who use. Instead of replacing their divots, they'd smoke them.

■

The only place you want grass on a golf course is under your ball.

■

Professional golfers can't use that stuff because they have to play in all kinds of weather. If you're going to be struck by lightning, you'd like to know about it.
... not just think you got a good bargain when you bought that stuff.

■

Besides, when a golfer says he's going straight, he likes to be talking about his tee shots, not his social life.

WOMEN'S RIGHTS

Women are demanding equality, and it's awfully nice of them to be willing to give up that much power to get it.

■

Women pilots have won the right to go into combat now. Well, praise the Lord and pass the tube of lipstick.

■

Women can go into combat without any special training. They've had all those years of marriage to fall back on.

■

Women pilots now are just the same as the men . . . although I hope they hang different pin-ups inside their lockers.

■

Anybody who doubts that women can be as mean and as tough as men should watch more women's tennis.

■

When you see a pilot with that long white scarf blowing in the wind, look more closely. It could be a loose brassiere.

■

Women can be just as mean and as tough as anybody in the military. Remember, they have to eat the same food.

■

Women have been trained for years to be tough in combat. You don't see too many of them coming out second best in divorce settlements.

■

Some feel that men are inherently more intelligent than women. Men don't give bridal and baby showers.

■

Women want to be treated the same as men. But some say if we all go into the next room for a cigar after dinner, how will the dishes ever get done?

Winston Churchill boosted the women's movement with his reply to an interviewer's question of "What do you say to the prediction that in the year 2000, women will be ruling the world?" Churchill smiled his smile and said, "They still will, eh?"

Chapter 11

GOVERNMENT AGENCIES

THE MILITARY

I know why the military travel on their stomachs. Their backs are too sore from sleeping on those mattresses.

■

The military has some food that is so dangerous the recipe was declared top secret.

... There's no telling what might happen if a navy cook's chili fell into enemy hands.

■

Women are allowed in combat now. Up until now, the only combat women have been allowed in is marriage.

■

Anybody who thinks women can't fight has never been to a January white sale.

Women make excellent fighters. If you don't believe me, invite two of them to a party sometime wearing the same dress.

■

Sleeping quarters in the military are kind of cramped. Just this morning I woke up with someone else's tattoo.

■

The first thing they do with cadets is shave their hair off. That's so that when they meet their drill sergeant for the first time, it doesn't stand on end.

■

Drill sergeants are all in excellent shape. Though, of course, it's easy to stay trim when all you eat is human blood.

■

The modern army is a little different. If it moves, you salute it; if it doesn't move, you promote it.

■

Drill sergeants are tough. Instead of a heart, they have a pet rock.

■

I like traveling with the military. You never lose your luggage. That's because you travel in the same compartment it does.

■

I don't know who invented the enlisted men's sleeping quarters, but I think it's the same man who invented the club sandwich.

■

They don't have to worry about comfortable sleeping quarters anyway. The military has it worked out so that as soon as they get comfortable in bed, it's time for them to be on duty anyway.

■

The cooks don't have to be good in the navy. It's very hard to tell food poisoning from seasickness.

■

The meals get pretty bad at sea. They threw some leftovers overboard the other night, and the sharks threw it back.

They tried to improve military cooking by changing the name for mess hall to dining hall. I don't know how they ever got that by the truth-in-advertising people.

■

Mess cooks have a famous saying, "If it moves, salute it; if it doesn't move, throw it in the stew."

■

They have top secrets in the Defense Department—like what prices they really paid for things.

■

If they want to punish the enemy, they don't have to fire shells at them. Just invite them onboard for dinner.

■

They serve that kind of food intentionally on board military ships. It makes seasickness feel like an improvement.

■

I asked one soldier if he had to march much and he said, "I don't know, but when I enlisted I had feet."

■

The military is anxious to please. The first thing they ask new recruits is, "How do you want your uniform—too big or too small?"

■

The military revolves around these four simple rules:
1. If it moves, salute it.
2. If it doesn't move, sweep it up.
3. If it's too big to sweep up, pick it up.
4. If it's too big to pick up, paint it.

■

The sergeant yelled to his recruits, "All right, you idiots, fall out!"

The group fell out . . . all but one. The sergeant stared at the young man, who smiled at him and said, "There were a lot of them, weren't there, Sarge?"

———————————■———————————

I'm still recovering from a shock. I was nearly drafted. It's not that I mind fighting for my country, but they called me at a ridiculous time: in the middle of a war.

—Jackie Mason

I was classified 4P by the draft board. In event of a war, I become a hostage.

—Woody Allen

You know what officer candidate school is? That's a concentration camp on our side.

—Bob Hope

Military intelligence is a contradiction in terms.

—Groucho Marx

You know what the Pentagon is? That's a big building in Washington that has five sides—on almost every issue.

—Henny Youngman

NASA

No one really knows how large space is or how much money it will absorb.

■

The government's latest space shuttle cost $1.8 billion. That's a lot of money. You could almost put a baseball team together for that much.
. . . Provided you go with a weak pitching staff.

■

The space shuttle cost $1.8 billion. Of course, it comes equipped with factory air, AM-FM stereo, and whitewall tires.
. . . A racing stripe down the side costs $180 extra.

The government just unveiled their latest space shuttle called the *Endeavor,* which means "to try." I don't like spending $1.8 billion for anything that has the word "try" in it.

... For that much dough I want the word "succeed" in there.

■

The latest space shuttle is supposed to be the finest spaceship ever built. We'd hate to pay $1.8 billion for mediocrity.

■

The latest space shuttle is supposed to be the Rolls Royce of space shuttles. That means in this one the toilet works.

We've had a lot of trouble with the toilets in space. Which I guess just proves that rocket scientists don't necessarily make good plumbers.

■

NASA has had a lot of plumbing problems with their space shuttles. The catch phrase among the astronauts used to be A-okay" now it's "Can you hold it until you get home?"

■

It's a real problem, though. Do you know how hard it is to keep your legs crossed without gravity?

■

Having plumbing problems really makes for a tough trip. Once you get out in space you can't stop at a Texaco restroom.

■

NASA has had several trips where they've had all that electronic gadgetry work perfectly and what they really needed was a can of Drano.

■

NASA has had so many plumbing problems that on the future trips they may send astronauts and a Roto-Rooter man.

■

This newest space shuttle comes with all the latest mechanical improvements ... except an air bag.

... NASA feels they already have enough of those in Washington.

The United States is determined to continue to explore outer space. I don't know what we're looking for up there, but I guess we'll know it when we see it.

■

NASA is really something, though. Something goes wrong with their spaceships that cost $32 million, and they call it a "glitch."
... I break out in glitches just thinking about $32 million.

■

One thing that's good about NASA is that it's completely nonpartisan. Democrats use up as much fuel as Republicans.

■

I still think walking in space is incredible. It's nice to go for a walk someplace where you don't have to worry about muggers.

■

With today's economy, NASA may have to search around for a no-frills space flight.
What they're doing now is looking around for an astronaut who can fly a space ship with a stick shift.

■

Instead of a regular space suit, you get a pair of long johns sprayed with silver paint.

■

And on this no-frills space flight, they won't send back television pictures. They'll just take a courtroom artist along with them.

■

It would take real teamwork to go to the moon under today's austerity program. The astronauts would have to figure out who would peddle and who would ride the handlebars.

■

No frills ... that's a polite way of saying "You better go to the restroom before you get on board."

■

Under this new austerity program, A-okay means "the last time we saw him, he was heading up."

NASA's cutting back on everything with today's austerity program. Of course, when the astronauts land on the moon the President still calls . . . provided they have enough left over to accept the charges.

■

You wonder why NASA doesn't send a doctor on every space flight. They found out it's too expensive. Everytime he talks to mission control, he sends them a bill.

■

Of course, they did send a doctor on one space flight. He was a real doctor, too. He was 13 minutes late for the blast-off.

He was the first astronaut to ever carry a phone beeper.

■

It's not easy for NASA to send a doctor into space. Most of them won't even make housecalls.

■

When NASA did send a doctor into space, they took a lot of precautions to keep him from getting homesick for his office. They sent along a stethoscope and a whole collection of 1948 magazines.

■

NASA is thinking of taking passengers along on some of their space flights. The cost would be $278,000 and $2.00 for the headsets.

■

A lot of people are anxious to go, too. They're busy now trying to figure out how they can write it off as a business trip.

■

A little word of warning for potential passengers though. If you go along on the space flight, don't get fresh with the stewardesses . . . unless you want to spend the rest of your life as a meteor.

■

A space trip would be very appealing to a lot of citizens. They'd love to be out there where there's no weight, no atmosphere, no taxes . . .

NASA is getting very serious about taking passengers along on their trips. They've installed a quarter insurance machine on one of their launching pads.

■

Passengers should check the flight out very carefully before signing up. That's a long way to go if the movies are lousy.

■

Even some of the commercial airlines are getting ready to book passage to the moon. They've already sent my luggage there twice.

■

For many years the United States space program encountered many difficulties. Bob Hope had this to say after we had another unsuccessful rocket ship fall into the ocean, "Well, I guess you've heard the good news from Cape Canaveral. The United States just launched another submarine."

■

What was John Glenn feeling moments before lifting off into space? "I looked around me and suddenly realized that everything had been built by the lowest bidder."

THE POST OFFICE

If you're fed up with slow postal service, write your Representative and hope it reaches him before reelection.

■

Some complain about our postal service, but it costs only 29 cents to mail a letter. That's only about a penny a day.

■

Sure, maybe the mails are slow, but in some places it's still faster than getting a dial tone.

■

Poor postal service has some advantages. It's the perfect excuse for not sending Christmas cards.

Congress has the perfect answer for speeding up the mail—deliver the letters by seniority.

■

Imagine paying more money for our postal service. That's like putting a coin meter on an outhouse.

■

There are some advantages to the slow mails. Mail carriers aren't bothered by dogs. By the time the letter arrives, the dog has lost all its teeth anyway.

■

Our postal service is obsolete, but they still keep raising the prices anyway. That's like a doctor starting to charge more for bloodletting.

■

Smart people are investing their money in stamps. They seem to go up faster than anything else.

■

How come the post office puts out gummed stamps, but we're the ones that take the licking?

■

Everything at the post office keeps going up. Hey, why don't we let them run the stock market?

■

The price of stamps is robbery. The post office should put their own picture up on their wall.

■

The post office is feeling guilty about how much they're charging. The new stamp is going to have John Dillinger's picture on it.

■

I prefer the days of the Pony Express . . . when the post office was run by complete horses.

■

Since the last rate increase the post office claims to have lost over 130 million. We're not sure whether that's dollars or letters.

The best way to beat the high cost of postage is to get friendly with your Avon lady. Then while she's going door to door, she can drop off your letters.

■

Postage is getting too expensive. For short notes now, it's cheaper to just hire a skywriter.

■

The high cost of postage is presenting hardships to some people. Kids in college can no longer afford to write home for money.

■

Pen pals will be a thing of the past. It'll be cheaper to just have the people come live with you.

■

Postal rates are getting a little excessive. My mailman now delivers the mail with a stocking pulled over his face.

■

If you don't like the increase in postal rates, write to your Congressman. It won't do you any good, but the post office can use the cash.

■

The greeting card industry gets furious over postal-rate increases. They always send the post office a nasty poem.

■

If the post office raises the rates much more, the mail carriers will be safe from dogs. It'll be the customers that bite them.

■

But you know, the post office will send a letter to Walla Walla, Washington; Des Moines, Iowa; Poughkeepsie, New York all for the small fee of about 30 cents. Big deal! When you fly to Chicago, Illinois, the airlines do that with your luggage for free.

■

If postal rates keep going up, it's soon going to be cheaper to send out Christmas telegrams.

If the cost of stamps gets up over 30 cents, licking them will not only be necessary, it will also be expressing an opinion.

■

As Joe Hickman puts it, "Communism is collapsing, and just when Americans thought we wouldn't have anyone to hate anymore—the Postal Service is raising stamps to 30 cents."

■

The post office is 200 years old. If I were that old, I'd move slowly too.

Chapter 12

GOVERNMENT GONE AWRY

FILIBUSTERS

A filibuster is a bag of hot air dressed up to look like a politician.

■

A filibuster is like asking Howard Cosell, "What did you think of the game?"

■

A filibuster is a nontelevised version of the Phil Donohue Show.

■

A filibuster is when politicians talk constantly so they won't have to act. It's very similar to their campaign strategy.

. . . and in many cases, their entire tenure in office.

A filibuster is two of a politician's favorite activities rolled into one—talking and saying nothing.

■

A filibuster is just a politician's way of taking three hours to say "no comment."

■

In Washington they call it a filibuster. On the evening weather reports they call it a "warm mass of hot air."

■

If you've ever seen those dryers in restrooms where you push a button and nothing but hot air comes out, you know what a filibuster is.

■

You've heard the expression, "It's an ill wind that blows no good?" That pretty much defines a filibuster.
. . . except this ill wind has to be elected.

■

There's only one person who can speak louder than a senator, and that's another senator.

IMMORALITY AMONG POLITICIANS

We've had a few politicians who have been involved in sexual scandals. They should have learned that a politician is supposed to straddle fences, not voters.

■

One high-ranking senator liked to womanize. They said of him he put his pants on the same as you and I . . . except a lot more often.

■

You know a politician is involved in a little hanky panky when he throws his hat in the ring and his trousers accidentally go with it.

Some of our elected officials do like their women. A few of them have campaigned to have the Congressional Record printed with a centerfold.

■

Then, too, some of our elected officials are dedicated to their sworn duty. They're the ones who have secretaries who can type. That's why Congress was moving so slowly for awhile. They could pass new bills in 3 days, but it took 14 days for them to find someone to type it up.

■

Sometimes it's good to have politicians who fool around with women. At least you know where their hands are.

■

I like to see politicians busy with affairs. It keeps them out of ours.

■

We've even had some candidates who were womanizers. If they got elected, the presidential song would be changed from "Hail to the Chief" to "Lover Come Back to Me."

■

A few of our presidential candidates had mistresses. If elected we would have had a first lady and a first lady and a half.

■

There have been some sex scandals associated with Washington. For awhile there Congress was the only massage parlor you had to be elected to.
. . . and an election to the house not only had to be confirmed, but consummated.

■

I knew one girl who was refused a job in the congressional secretarial pool. Under "sex" on her application she wrote "female." The correct answer should have been "yes."

■

We've had several sex scandals in Washington in recent years. Besides an oath of office, they'd better start taking a vow of chastity.

For awhile there it was getting so bad that you couldn't send an elected official to Washington without a chaperone.

■

There have been several sex scandals in our Capitol. We should make it a law, no official can be sent to Washington without a hobby.

■

Every so many years we have another sex scandal in Washington. Doesn't that town have any cold showers?

■

No wonder politicians work so hard to get elected. It's cheaper than getting your own dates.

■

Lily Tomlin feels that "98% of the adults in this country are decent, hard-working, honest Americans. It's the other lousy 2% that get all the publicity. But then—we elected them."

■

According to Bob Orben, if the ten commandments were left to politicians they would have read: "Thou shalt not (unless you feel strongly to the contrary)."

■

A prominent member of Congress once was pleading his case before some hostile voters. A heavy stone was thrown at him, which, as he happened to stoop at that instant, passed over his head.

"You see," he said to his friends, "if I had been an upright politician, I would have been killed."

■

If some of our government officials had their conscience taken out, it would be minor surgery.

CRIME IN OFFICE

We've had periods of a lot of crime by elected officials. For awhile there when they took roll call in Congress the proper response was either "present" or "not guilty."

Some of our representatives have been guilty of so much that when they finally left office, we retired their prison numbers.

■

A few of our elected officials have been thieves from the beginning. Right after they administered the oath of office, the Bible was missing.

■

Occasionally we send a bad apple to Washington. Once in awhile you get a guy who goes from the oath of office right into the fifth amendment.

■

Some people forget ours is a government *of* the people, *by* the people, and *for* the people. They get in office and just do it *to* the people.

■

We should suspect some of the people we elect. Like the one guy who gave his entire acceptance while holding his hat over his face.

■

One elected official was shocked when he was taken to police headquarters, photographed, fingerprinted, and told to empty his pockets. It was the first time he had ever had his hands in his own pockets.

■

It's to be expected from time to time. After all, politicians are only human—despite what they say in their campaign speeches.

■

Every once in a while a politician gets caught with his hand in the cookie jar. It wouldn't bother any of us so much if we were allowed to pay our taxes with cookies.

■

A lot of politicians were born with silver spoons in their mouths, but the spoons probably had hotel names on them.

■

According to Bob Hope we've had at least one President who didn't fall into this category. Mr. Hope said "Ronald Reagan is not a typical politician because he doesn't know how to lie, cheat, and steal. He's always had an agent for that."

■

We all know that half the people in Washington are crooks. The real experts are the ones who know which half.

CONGRESSIONAL HEARINGS

Congressional hearings are dull. There should be a law against putting that many politicians and that many microphones in one room.

■

Those Congressional hearings would be a lot more fun if they'd have Pat Sajak asking the questions and Vanna White handing out the prizes.

. . . of course, that wouldn't work. Everytime Vanna turned over a letter, they'd deny it.

■

Congressional hearings are fun to watch on TV. They look like "The People's Court" with an all-star cast.

■

Congressional hearings are as tough on the committee as they are on the person being questioned. They have to sit up there all day and look honest.

■

At the swearing-in for these hearings they ask, "Do you swear to tell the truth, the whole truth, and nothing but the truth." The answer is, "If I did, would I be in politics?"

■

Political hearings are fun. These people once took an oath of office swearing not to do the things they're now swearing to tell the truth about.

The American people love scandals, though. We love it when they throw the newspaper on the front porch and the front page is smoking.

■

And no one can ever remember anything when they're being questioned. These hearings all prove just one thing: When you go into politics, your memory goes, too.

■

The people who are on the committee at these hearings have an almost impossible job. They're trying to give politics a good name.

■

Harry Truman offered this advice concerning committee hearings: "Generals should never do anything that needs to be explained to a Senate committee—there is nothing one can explain to a Senate committee.

■

A Senate committee must consist of at least five people. One who does the work, three others to pat him on the back, and one to bring in a minority report.

■

Congressional hearings are ironic. Imagine . . . they're trying to get to the truth and they're in politics.

■

I love the way the politicians on official hearings are so polite even though they can't stand each other's guts. It's kind of like a virus being polite to penicillin.

■

It's fun watching Congressional hearings on TV. It's nice seeing politicians asking for the truth for a change . . . instead of money.

■

Some of the committee members have to ask the same question five or six different ways before they finally understand the answer. It must be tough for a politician who has to go real bad trying to find out where the rest room is.

■

Watching some of these people, you wonder why we ever sent them to Washington. In fact, you wonder how they ever found their way.

CONGRESSIONAL INVESTIGATIONS

I remember one time Congress was investigating lousy airline service. If anyone should know about lousy service, it's them.

■

I love the political witnesses. They swear to tell the truth, the whole truth, and nothing but the truth . . . unless it's already been shredded.

■

To me, these investigations are confusing. I watched 7 different witnesses and heard 8 versions of what happened.
. . . one witness was bipartisan.

■

People watch these Congressional investigations and are divided. Ten percent think the accused is a villain. Ten percent think the accused is a hero. And the other 80 percent are just mad at the accused because he's making them miss their soap opera.

■

Some people think watching congressional investigations makes for dull television. Well, the soap operas would be dull, too, if everyone on them were under oath.

■

Congressional investigations are a different kind of television. You answer questions, but you don't get any prizes.
. . . unless you consider "ten to twenty" a prize.

I like to see all those members of Congress sitting in on these investigations that drag on forever. It keeps them from passing more laws.

■

A lot of the witnesses at these investigations say they knew nothing about what was going on in Washington ... and they have their voting record to back that up.

■

All government investigations can be summed up by the old saying, "After all is said and done, more is said than done."

■

There are so many investigations. This could be because every man has his price, and so many are holding bargain sales.

INDEX

L

M

N

O

P

R

Rabble rousers, 13-14
Raises, 5
Rather, Dan, 100
Raye, Martha, 40
Reagan, Ronald, 72, 73, 74,
    102, 107, 175-76
Receptionists, 47-48
Recession, 140-43
Republicans, 80-81
Restaurants
    maitre d's, 59-60
    waiters, 60-61
Retirement
    clock watcher and, 9
    goldbricker and, 11
Rogers, Will, 67, 70, 74, 76, 78,
    79, 80, 100, 114, 116
Ross, Diana, 79, 98
Roosevelt, Franklin Delano, 72
Rumor mongers, 14-15
Russia, 98-99, 121
Ruth, Babe, 142-43

S

Sahl, Mort, 70
Sajak, Pat, 176
Salisbury, Lord, 80
Secretaries, 46-47
Security officers, airport, 55-57
Senate, 77-79
Sex
    coffee and, 19-20
    golf and, 51-52
    politics and, 172-73
Shaw, George Bernard, 60, 116

Show business, and politics,
    105-7
Slob, 36-37
Smoker, 29-30
Space program, 162-66
Sports
    drugs and, 153
    football, 11, 135, 136, 150
    gambling, 135-36
Stevenson, Adlai, 74
Sunshine spreader, 12-13
Supreme Court, 79-80

T

Tardiness, 5-7
Taxes, 109-15, 132
Taylor, Elizabeth, 101
Television
    election returns, 100-101
    evangelists, 94
"They," 43-44
Tomlin, Lily, 174
Traffic cops, 53-55
Trebek, Alex, 79
Trivia nut, 32-33
Troublemakers, 13-14
Truman, Harry, 72, 177
Trump, Donald, 119
TV evangelists, 94
Twain, Mark, 78, 79, 113
Two-party system, 80-81

U

Unemployment, 145-46
Unhappy co-worker, 23-24
Unlucky worker, 22-23